THE INN AT RANCHO SANTA FE

Celebrating 50 Years of Ownership
by the Royce Family

PRESENTS

CHEF JOHN BERIKER

EAST MEETS WEST

FRENCH CALIFORNIA AND MEDITERRANEAN CUISINE

THE FINEST AND FRESHEST LOCAL INGREDIENTS

Written by Maria Desiderata Montana

Photography by Vincent Knakal

Design by Andrea Jewel Allison

The Inn

Copyright © 2008 by John Beriker
Photographs © 2008 by Vincent Knakal
All rights reserved
Published in the United States by The Inn at Rancho Santa Fe
Printed in the United States by Precision Litho

Historical photos provided by The Inn at Rancho Santa Fe

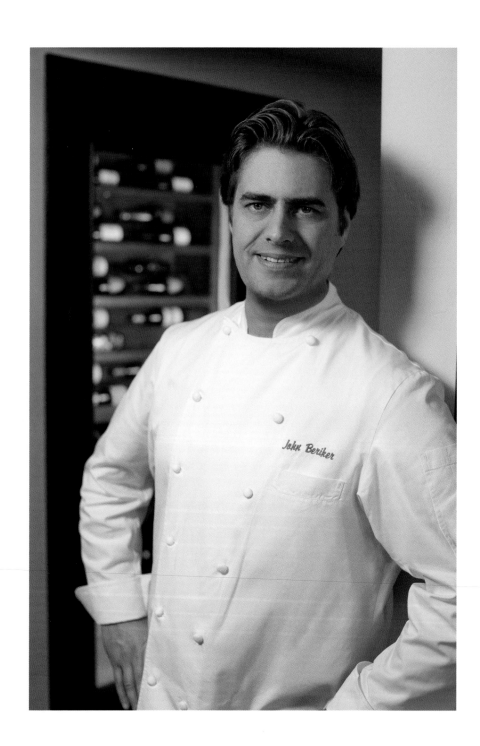

EXECUTIVE CHEF JOHN BERIKER

The Inn at Rancho Santa Fe
Biography

For over twenty years, John Beriker has been impressing clients, peers and critics with his unique fusion of classic French California and Asian cuisine. His modern and cutting edge 'East meets West' cuisine has gained him critical acclaim by some of the most respected culinary experts in the world. Working directly with his long-time mentor, the world-renowned Wolfgang Puck at Spago in Hollywood, California, provided a strong base from which he launched his Executive Chef career. According to Wolfgang Puck, Beriker is "one of the world's leading chefs with extraordinary ability and brilliant talent."

Beriker has graced the kitchens in some of the finest hotels and restaurants all over the world, including an Executive Chef Position and co-ownership with brothers James and Timur at award-winning Rustica restaurant in Beverly Hills. He was the Executive Chef at Raffles International Hotel J.P. Bastiani in Singapore and a member of The Raffles Culinary Academy, where he organized cooking demonstrations and luncheons. Beriker was Executive Chef at the prestigious Hotel Vier Jahreszeiten in Hamburg, Germany and the opening Executive Chef of the Merchant Court Hotel in Sydney, Australia. He also reigned supreme as the Executive Chef at the Auberge Dab and Park Avenue in Bangkok, Thailand.

Beriker received critical acclaims and awards, including 'Best Dining Experience' by the Singapore Tourist Promotion Board in 1996 and 'Best New Chef of the Year' by Gault Millau in Hamburg, Germany in 1999. He has been widely and positively recognized with multiple reviews in magazines; namely Wine & Dine Magazine of Singapore, as well as other major magazines, newspapers, and trade journals in Singapore, Australia, Germany and the U.S.A.

At present, Beriker is a member of the Chaîne des Rôtisseurs and Executive Chef at The Inn at Rancho Santa Fe where he supervises all the planning and preparation of menus, meals, banquets and outside catering. As a culinary artist, he displays his passion for cooking by igniting a bounty of fresh seasonal ingredients into simple dishes that are unsurpassed in beauty and flavor. Beriker loves the "WOW" factor that his guests often exclaim when tasting his cuisine. "I wanted to create a cookbook that people can get excited about," he says. "I want the reader to see the picture of what beautiful dish they are about to re-create and, after reading over the recipe, know that they can make that dish and enjoy!"

Stephen W. Royce pitcher for the
New York Giants

Three generations of the Royce family

View from The Inn 1924.

HISTORY OF THE INN

The Inn at Rancho Santa Fe remains a historic landmark of beauty and legendary hospitality, setting the standard for perfection and opulence with its Spanish and Mediterranean style décor and a 23-acre lush landscape. Winding cobblestone pathways connect private cottages of luxuriously appointed guest rooms and suites for unsurpassed deluxe accommodations.

Historic Rancho Santa Fe began over a century ago as a Mexican land grant given in gratitude to San Diego's first mayor Juan Osuna. In the early 1900's, the Osuna family sold 6,000 acres of Rancho San Dieguito to the Santa Fe railroad to plant a Eucalyptus forest. When the wood proved unsuitable for railroad ties, the railroad commissioned architect, Lilian Rice to design a community around a quaint village and a guest house for prospective land purchasers. The town was named Rancho Santa Fe and in 1922 Lilian Rice designed The Inn as a twelve-room California Mission-style adobe guest house for visitors, with a small dining room. By 1923 this small hotel was renamed "La Morada" (Spanish for the home with many rooms) and opened to the public.

Meet the management of

the *Inn* at *Rancho Santa Fe*

Drop in soon
for luncheon
or dinner
and see
the family at work!

Mr. Stephen Royce, general manager. Mr. Royce (Dorothy's dad, and grandfather to all the Hadden children) has taken over the management of the Inn. For many years Mr. Royce was owner and manager of the Huntington Hotel in Pasadena.

Mrs. Dorothy Hadden arranges flowers in the attractive, spacious lobby. Her talents in flower arrangement brighten every corner of the Inn, especially on each of the tables in the dining room.

Duncan Hadden, assistant to the manager. He is a June, 1970 graduate of the University of Puget Sound and will make his career in hotel management.

When you call the Inn these days, you will be greeted by the friendly "hello" of Marian Hadden. During the fall she is a student at Bishops. Her summer job keeps her very busy as she handles all the duties belonging to a switchboard operator.

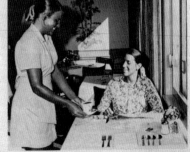

Marne Hadden is a waitress in the dining room. When the school bells ring in the fall, she will return to Pine Manor, Chestnut Hill, Mass. as a sophomore.

◁ Jane Hadden is only eight years old, but her duties are very important. Every morning (when the dew is still on the roses) she prunes each bush for dead leaves and flowers.

Lynn Hadden's duties are as a relief maid—which covers a great deal of territory as she will testify! She is a recent graduate from Briarcliffe college, Briarcliff, New York.

The Inn 1970

Stephen W. Royce

La Morada evolved gracefully into The Inn at Rancho Santa Fe
including ownership by George Roslington in the 1930's, and Mr.
and Mrs. George Richardson in 1941. Stephen Wheeler Royce
(1892-1977), renowned for establishing the Huntington Hotel as
one of the most celebrated hotels in the United States, had a vision
of how spectacular The Inn could become in the future. He followed
his vision and purchased The Inn at Rancho Santa Fe in 1958. Prior
to that, Royce attended Hamilton College in Clinton, New York. After spending one season as a pitcher for the New York Giants, Royce
earned his law degree from the New York Law School. During World
War I, Royce served as an officer in the Army Air Force.

The Inn at Rancho Santa Fe has earned an eminent place in the
hearts of residents and visitors, including celebrities and royalty,
due to the loyalty, dedication and guidance of the Royce family who
have ensured The Inn's time-honored opulence, charm and integ-
rity. The Inn became known throughout the country due to listings
in 'Distinguished Hotels of America', 'Country Inns of America', and
'Historical Hotels of America'. Conde Nast Johansens, the interna-
tionally acclaimed publisher of hotel guides, has recommended The
Inn at Rancho Santa Fe in its 2008 Guide to Recommended Hotels,
Inns and Resorts for North America.

This year of 2008 marks fifty years of The Inn's continuous ownership represented by Duncan Royce Hadden; who managed The Inn
for ten years, Stephen Royce and Dede Vlietstra. In celebration of
their fifty year anniversary, the Royce Family together with Chairman of the Board Murray Hutchison, Board Member Dan Pittard,
and Managing Director Kerman Beriker, with son and Executive Chef
John Beriker, are proud to present this cookbook as a historical
memoir and cherished keepsake.

Board Members, top row: left to right; Dan Pittard, Stephen Royce, Duncan Royce Hadden, Managing Director Kerman Beriker. Bottom row: Dede Vlietstra, Chairman of the Board Murray Hutchison

Contents

appetizers

SMOKED **Salmon Napoleon**

Foie Gras WITH WATERCRESS

Crab Tower WITH CILANTRO COULIS

Salmon POCKET

Spring Rolls WITH PORK

Jumbo Scallop WITH DRAGON FRUIT

Shrimp Tempura WITH SAMBAL CHILI SAUCE

ORGANIC **Cucumber Martini**

Salmon TARTAR

CHILLED **Tomato Terrine**

Provencal Tart WITH GRUYÈRE CHEESE

White Asparagus IN HOLLANDAISE SAUCE

King Prawns WITH CUCUMBER

PEPPER CRUSTED **Skate Wings**

Langostinos AND ROOT VEGETABLE CHIPS

Baked Snails WITH CREAMED SPINACH

Fresh Mozzarella AND COLORED PEPPERS

Smoked Salmon Napoleon

SERVES SIX

18 smoked salmon strips (pre-packaged), finely julienned
3 teaspoons extra-virgin olive oil, divided
3 teaspoons black sesame seeds
3 teaspoons white toasted sesame seeds
2 tablespoons sesame oil
1 green onion, finely minced
2 teaspoons fresh ginger root, finely chopped
Sea salt
White pepper
8 large red tomatoes, cored
4 carrots, roughly chopped
2 yellow onions, peeled and halved
1 package taro chips, any flavor

SMOKED SALMON MIXTURE
In a large bowl, combine salmon, 2 teaspoons olive oil, sesame seeds, sesame oil, green onions, ginger root and salt and pepper, to taste. Toss well to combine.

RED TOMATO COULIS
Preheat the oven to 400 F. Grease a baking dish with 1 teaspoon of olive oil. Arrange tomatoes, carrots and onions in baking dish. Lightly sprinkle with salt and pepper, to taste. Roast until tender, about 15 to 20 minutes. Cool. Remove skin from the tomatoes. Transfer the ingredients in small batches to a blender and puree until very smooth. Strain the mixture through a sieve into a large bowl.

CREATE YOUR PLATE
Create three layers. Ladle tomato coulis in the center of a plate or bowl. Place a spoonful of salmon mixture on top of the coulis. Top with a taro chip. Repeat 2 more times.

Chef's Tip:

You don't have to use taro chips. Get creative and substitute any flavor and style of chip that you like best!

14

FOIE GRAS WITH WATERCRESS

SERVES SIX

2 pounds foie gras (duck liver)
Sea salt
White pepper
1 cup all-purpose flour, more if needed
½ cup extra-virgin olive oil
½ cup lemon juice
1 shallot, minced
3 cups watercress
½ cup butter
½ cup sugar
1 large apple cut into 18 thin slices

FOIE GRAS

Slice foie gras into 1/4 inch slices and season both sides with salt and pepper. Place the flour in a bowl. Coat both sides of the foie gras with flour. Heat a large sauté pan over high heat. Place the foie gras in the pan and cook until golden brown, about 1 to 2 minutes on each side. *Note: keep the pan still and do not move it while cooking the foie gras. The foie gras should be crispy on the outside and soft in the middle. Remove the foie gras from the pan and drain on paper towels.

LEMON AND OLIVE OIL DRESSING

In a large bowl, whisk olive oil, lemon juice, and shallots.

WATERCRESS SALAD

Add watercress to a large bowl. Drizzle lemon and olive oil dressing on top. Add salt and pepper, to taste. Toss gently.

CARAMELIZED APPLES

In a small saucepan over medium-high heat, melt butter and sugar. Add apple slices and cook until caramelized, about 2 to 3 minutes.

CREATE YOUR PLATE

Arrange watercress onto the center of a plate. Place foie gras on top. Garnish with 3 caramelized apple slices.

Chef's Tip:

Foie gras is one of the most popular and well-known delicacies in French cuisine because it is rich, buttery, and delicate. Therefore, do not add any oil or cooking spray to the sauté pan when cooking. The foie gras basically cooks itself in its own natural oils.

CRAB TOWER WITH CILANTRO COULIS

SERVES SIX

Chef's Tip:

Prepare this dish only when ready to serve so that the rice crackers don't get soggy. Use any crackers of you choice.

6 cups fresh crabmeat, finely chopped
1 red bell pepper, seeded and finely minced
1 yellow bell pepper, seeded and finely minced
1 green bell pepper, seeded and finely minced
3 shallots, finely minced
1 cup mayonnaise
4 tablespoons freshly squeezed lemon juice, divided
½ cup bread crumbs
Sea salt
White pepper
1 cup fresh cilantro
½ cup plain yogurt
½ cup sour cream
18 mini rice crackers
3 ripe avocados, peeled, pitted and cut into 18 slices

CRAB SALAD
In a large bowl, combine crabmeat, peppers, shallots, mayonnaise, 2 tablespoons lemon juice, bread crumbs and salt and pepper, to taste.

CILANTRO COULIS
In a blender, combine cilantro, yogurt, sour cream, 2 tablespoons lemon juice and salt and pepper, to taste. Puree until smooth.

CREATE YOUR PLATE
Ladle cilantro coulis onto the bottom of a plate, top with crabmeat mixture, and layer 1 cracker on the top. Repeat 2 more times. Garnish with 3 avocado slices.

Salmon Pocket

Serves Six

2 salmon fillets (about 6 ounces each), deboned, skinned and finely chopped
1-1/2 cups sour cream, divided
2 tablespoons wasabi powder
1 tablespoon soy sauce
Sea salt
White pepper
½ cup beet root juice
½ cup yogurt
18 slices smoked salmon (pre-packaged)
6 four-inch molds
12 tablespoons black caviar or salmon roe
6 wontons

SALMON FILLING
In a large bowl combine finely chopped salmon fillets, 1 cup sour cream, wasabi powder, soy sauce, and salt and pepper, to taste.

BEET ROOT CREAM
In a small bowl combine beet root juice, yogurt and ½ cup of sour cream. Whisk until smooth.

SALMON PREPARATION
Place 3 smoked salmon slices inside a 4 inch mold, making sure half of the edges are folded over the sides. Spoon salmon filling inside the mold. Lightly overlap the salmon strips, carefully folding over the mold. Repeat for remaining 5 molds.

CREATE YOUR PLATE
Turn the mold upside down onto a plate. Drizzle beet root cream around the plate. Place black caviar on top and garnish with a wonton.

Chef's Tip:

Substitute wonton garnish for anything you like.

Spring Rolls with Pork

Serves Six (18 Spring Rolls)

1 bag glass noodles
1 whole cabbage, shredded
1 large carrot, shredded
3 celery stalks, finely julienned
10 shitake mushrooms, julienned
3 tablespoons extra-virgin olive oil
6 cloves crushed garlic
8 cups ground pork
Sea salt
White pepper
30 spring roll sheets (4x4 inches)
8 cups cornstarch
Canola oil, for deep-frying
2 cups granulated sugar
2 cups soy sauce
4 cups sweet and sour Thai chili sauce
2 limes, juiced
2 tablespoons finely chopped ginger

Chef's Tip:

Substitute minced prawns or chicken for the pork

NOODLES AND VEGETABLES
Soak the glass noodles in warm water for about 5 to 10 minutes until soft. Drain and cut noodles to 1 inches in length. In a large bowl, combine glass noodles with cabbage, carrots, celery and mushrooms.

PORK
In a wok, sauté olive oil and garlic until fragrant. Add ground pork and fry until cooked, about 3 minutes. Remove from heat.

In a large bowl, combine noodle and vegetable mixture with pork mixture. Season with salt and pepper, to taste. Mix well.

THAI DIPPING SAUCE
In a large bowl combine sugar, soy sauce, Thai chili sauce, lime juice and ginger. Mix well.

EGG ROLLS

Place a teaspoon of the filling in the center of a spring roll sheet. Reserve 1 inch of empty sheet on each side of the filling and fold it towards the center to cover the filling. Roll the sheet with the filling in to the shape of a cigar. Lightly dredge egg rolls in cornstarch. Heat the canola oil in a very large, deep pot or heat an electric fryer to 360 degrees F. Fry the egg rolls, in batches, until crispy and golden brown. Drain on paper towels.

CREATE YOUR PLATE

Arrange spring rolls on a serving platter. Slice the very ends of each roll diagonally, so the ingredients inside are visible. Fill oriental spoons with dipping sauce and arrange around the sides of the platter.

JUMBO SCALLOP WITH DRAGON FRUIT

SERVES SIX

6 Scallops (U-8) (2 ounces each)
Sea salt
White pepper
3 tablespoons extra-virgin olive oil
¼ cup white wine
2 whole shallots, minced
1 tablespoon cilantro leaves
1 tablespoon white wine vinegar
1 large lime, juiced
2 whole dragon fruits, peeled and julienned
1 16 ounce can frozen orange juice concentrate
½ cup granulated sugar
3 tablespoons miso paste
2 tablespoons rice wine vinegar
2 1/2 cup mirin (sweet rice cooking wine)

SCALLOPS

Lightly season scallops on both sides with salt and pepper, to taste. Heat olive oil in a large sauté pan over medium-high heat. Place scallops in the pan and cook until crispy, about 2 minutes on each side. Add white wine to seal in the flavor.

DRAGON FRUIT RELISH

In a large bowl, whisk shallots, cilantro, white wine vinegar and lime juice. Gently fold in dragon fruit.

ORANGE PINK PEPPERCORN MISO DRESSING

In a large bowl whisk orange juice, sugar, miso paste, rice wine vinegar and mirin.

CREATE YOUR PLATE

Spoon orange miso dressing onto the center of a plate. Place dragon relish on top of miso dressing. Top with 1 jumbo scallop.

Chef's Tip:

Do not whisk the dragon fruit because it is extremely fragile.

Shrimp Tempura with Sambal Chili Sauce

SERVES SIX

Canola oil, for frying
1 package tempura mix
12 shrimp (4-6 count)
½ cup Sambal chili sauce
3 tablespoons soy sauce
2 cups sweet chili sauce
3 tablespoons granulated sugar
2 limes, juiced

Heat the canola oil in a very large, deep pot or heat an electric fryer to 360 degrees F.

Chef's Tip:

To make the shrimp crispier, substitute cold seltzer water for tap water in the tempura batter.

TEMPURA BATTER
Make the tempura batter according to the package instructions. Lightly dredge the shrimp in the tempura batter. Fry the shrimp, in batches, until golden brown. Drain on paper towels.

SAMBAL CHILI SAUCE
In a medium-size bowl combine Sambal chili sauce, soy sauce, sweet chili sauce, sugar and lime juice. Whisk until blended.

CREATE YOUR PLATE
Spoon Sambal chili sauce into a small dipping bowl in the center of a round serving platter. Arrange shrimp around the platter. Serve family style.

26

ORGANIC CUCUMBER MARTINI

SERVES SIX

6 chilled martini glasses
6 whole organic cucumbers, peeled and cut into chunks
1 whole organic lemon, juiced
3 tablespoons fresh organic dill, divided
¾ cup crème fraîche

CUCUMBER PUREE
In a blender combine cucumbers, lemon juice and 1 tablespoon fresh dill. Puree until smooth. Transfer the mixture to a large bowl. Cover with plastic wrap and chill in the refrigerator for at least 1 hour.

CREATE YOUR GLASS
Ladle cucumber puree into chilled martini glasses. Drizzle with crème fraîche and garnish with the remaining 2 tablespoons of fresh dill.

Chef's Tip:

This is a non-alcoholic appetizer that is refreshing and delicious!

SALMON TARTAR

SERVES SIX

Chef's Tip:

You can also use fresh orange wedges as a garnish

1 pound raw salmon, finely chopped
7 teaspoons extra-virgin olive oil, divided
2 lemons, juiced
2 tablespoons Dijon mustard
2 tablespoons capers, chopped
2 shallots, finely minced
Sea salt
White pepper
6 round cookie cutters
4 large red radishes cut into 24 thin slices
1-11 ounce can Mandarin oranges, in light syrup

SALMON MIXTURE
In a large bowl, combine salmon, 1 teaspoon of olive oil, lemon juice, mustard, capers and shallots. Season with salt and pepper, to taste. Mix gently.

CREATE YOUR PLATE
Pack salmon mixture into 6 round cookie cutters. Flip upside down onto 6 individual plates. Garnish each plate with 4 radish slices and 3 Mandarin oranges (more if desired). Finish by drizzling 1 teaspoon of olive oil around each plate.

CHILLED TOMATO TERRINE

SERVES SIX

6 cups tomato juice
½ cup lemon juice
Sea Salt
White pepper
30 gelatin sheets
3 cups whole red pear tomatoes
3 cups whole yellow pear tomatoes
6 small gelatin molds of your choice
2 tablespoons extra-virgin olive oil
1 whole shallot, finely diced
2 cups white wine, chardonnay
1-1/2 cups butter, softened
1 cup guava puree
8 basil leaves, julienned

TOMATO MIXTURE
In a large saucepan over moderate heat, simmer tomato juice, lemon juice and salt and pepper, to taste. Add gelatin sheets, stirring constantly until the gelatin sheets completely dissolve. Set aside and cool. Evenly divide tomatoes, alternating colors, and place into each of the individual molds. Pour tomato gelatin mixture into each mold, making sure to completely cover the tomatoes. Refrigerate until set, about 2 hours.

WHITE WINE BEURRE BLANC SAUCE
In a small saucepan, heat olive oil over medium-high heat. Add shallots and sauté until tender, about 10 minutes. Slowly stir in white wine. Reduce heat and simmer, stirring often, until the mixture reduces by one-half, about 30 minutes. Cover sauce and cool to room temperature. Add butter and whisk until creamy.

GUAVA SAUCE
In a large bowl, combine beurre blanc sauce with guava puree. Mix well.

CREATE YOUR PLATE
Ladle guava sauce onto the center of a dinner plate. Lift the tomato terrine out of the mold and carefully place in the center of the guava sauce. Garnish with basil leaves.

Chef's Tip:

Line the individual gelatin molds with saran wrap before adding the tomatoes and juice.

PROVENCAL TART WITH GRUYÈRE CHEESE

SERVES SIX

1 sheet frozen puff pastry, thawed
All purpose flour, for dusting work surface
1 egg, well beaten
6 red onions, finely julienned
4 cups granulated sugar
2 bottles of port wine
3 cups hummus
3 cups Gruyère cheese
12 red heirloom tomatoes, cubed
12 yellow heirloom tomatoes, cubed
18 kalamata olives, whole
1 summer truffle cut into 18 paper thin slices (optional garnish)

Preheat oven to 350 degrees F. Line a baking sheet with wax paper.

Chef's Tips:

*Watch that
the pastry
doesn't burn.*

*Substitute any
store-bought
flavor marma-
lade that you
like best.*

PUFF PASTRY
On a lightly floured work surface, unroll the pastry dough. Using a
floured 6 inch cookie cutter, cut the pastry into 6 rounds and lightly
brush with egg mixture. Place pastry rounds on the baking sheet
and bake in the oven until puffed and golden brown in color, about
12 to 15 minutes. Remove from the oven and, using the tip of a par-
ing knife, cut out the center portion of each pastry.

RED ONION MARMALADE
In a large, heavy saucepan, combine onions, sugar and wine. Bring
to a boil and continue to simmer over medium-high heat until most
of the liquid has evaporated.

Preheat the oven to 250 degrees F.

Dividing ingredients into 6 portions, fill each pastry tart starting with the hummus first, followed by the cheese and tomatoes. Finish with 3 kalamata olives and top with more cheese. Gently place filled pastry tarts on a baking sheet. Bake until the cheese is fully melted, approximately 12 minutes.

CREATE YOUR PLATE

Remove pastries and place on 6 individual plates. Spoon red onion marmalade on top and around the edges of each tart.
Garnish with 3 shaved truffle slices per plate.

WHITE ASPARAGUS IN HOLLANDAISE SAUCE

SERVES SIX

18 large white asparagus spears
5 egg yolks
2 tablespoons fresh lemon juice
2 teaspoons Worcestershire sauce
4 cups clarified butter
Sea salt
White pepper

ASPARAGUS
Clean, peel, and trim the end of each asparagus spear. In a very large pot, add enough water to immerse the asparagus spears. Add salt to the water. Bring to a boil. Carefully drop in the asparagus spears and boil until just tender, about 3 minutes. Remove and place in a large bowl of ice-water.

HOLLANDAISE SAUCE
In a stainless steel bowl set over a pot of simmering water, whisk egg yolks, lemon juice and Worcestershire until smooth. Whisking vigorously, add the butter, 1 cup at a time, until all is incorporated. Season with salt and pepper, to taste.

CREATE YOUR PLATE
Ladle hollandaise sauce onto a serving platter. Carefully layer asparagus spears on top of the sauce. Drizzle more hollandaise sauce on top. Serve family style.

Chef's Tip:

If you want an added splash of color, garnish with diced red tomatoes or finely chopped Italian parsley....or both!

King Prawns with Cucumber

SERVES SIX

18 shrimp (13-15 count), peeled, cleaned and deveined
Sea salt
White pepper
3 tablespoons colored tobiko caviar (flying fish roe)
¼ cup plus 3 tablespoons extra-virgin olive oil, divided
¾ cup fresh squeezed lemon juice
2 tablespoons chives, finely chopped
4 red bell peppers
1 garlic clove, minced
3 Japanese cucumbers, peeled and shredded
9 quail eggs, hard-boiled, peeled and halved

SHRIMP
Bring a large pot of salted water to a boil. Add the shrimp and cook for about 3 minutes, stirring once or twice. Do not overcook. Remove immediately and chill in a large bowl of ice water.

TOBIKO SAUCE
In a small bowl, add caviar, ¼ cup olive oil, lemon juice, chives and salt and pepper, to taste. Mix well.

ROASTED BELL PEPPERS
Preheat oven to 425 degrees F. Cover a heavy baking sheet with foil and coat with cooking spray. Arrange peppers on baking sheet and bake until the skins brown and blister, turning the peppers over occasionally, about 20 to 25 minutes. Place peppers in a bowl, cover with plastic wrap and allow to cool; about 10 minutes. Peel, seed and cut peppers into strips. In a bowl, gently toss the pepper strips with 3 tablespoons olive oil, garlic and salt and pepper, to taste.

CREATE YOUR PLATE
Arrange peppers onto the center of a plate. Top with shredded cucumber. Place three prawns on top of cucumber. Arrange 3 quail egg (halves) around the plate. Finish with tobiko sauce.

Chef's Tip:

Provide an extra savory flavor to the shrimp by placing fresh peppercorns and bay leaves in the water before bringing it to a boil.

Pepper Crusted Skate Wings

6 whole tomatoes, cored
1 cup crushed pepper
½ cup grated fresh ginger
6 skate fillets, about 5 ounces each
8 tablespoons extra-virgin olive oil, divided
Sea salt
White pepper
2 whole shallots, finely diced
1 bottle red wine, merlot
3 cups butter, softened
18 kalamata olives

TOMATO PUREE
Preheat the oven to 425 degrees F. Line a baking sheet with foil and coat with cooking spray. Arrange tomatoes on baking sheet and roast for 20 to 25 minutes. Cool and remove skin. Transfer tomatoes in batches to a blender. Puree until smooth.

PEPPER-GINGER CRUST
In a medium-size bowl combine crushed pepper and ginger. Rub skate fillets on both sides with 2 tablespoons of olive oil and season with salt and pepper, to taste. Dip one side of each skate fillet into the pepper and ginger mixture, forming a layer of crust on the top. Heat 3 tablespoons of olive oil in a large sauté pan over medium-high heat. Place the skate fillets in the hot pan until cooked and golden brown, about 3 minutes per side.

RED WINE AND TOMATO BEURRE BLANC
Heat 3 tablespoons of olive oil in a large saucepan over moderate heat. Add shallots and sauté until tender, about 10 minutes. Slowly stir in red wine and tomato puree mixture. Simmer, stirring often, until the mixture reduces by one-half, about 30 minutes. Cover sauce and cool to room temperature. Whisk in butter, 1 cup at a time, stirring constantly until creamy. Strain the mixture through a sieve into a large bowl.

CREATE YOUR PLATE
Ladle a generous amount of the tomato beurre blanc sauce onto a large plate with a deep rim. Place 1 skate fillet on top. Scatter 3 kalamata olives around the plate.

LANGOSTINOS AND ROOT VEGETABLE CHIPS

SERVES SIX

18 langostinos (prawns, about 4 ounces each), cleaned and deveined
1 large eggplant, halved and scored
2 cloves fresh garlic, crushed
1 teaspoon extra-virgin olive oil
Sea salt
White pepper
2 tablespoons grated Parmigiano-Reggiano cheese
4 tablespoons freshly squeezed lemon juice, divided
1 sweet potato
1 lotus root
1 watermelon radish
Canola oil for frying
5 egg yolks
2 teaspoons Worcestershire sauce
4 cups clarified butter

Preheat oven to 350 degrees F. In a large pot, bring water to a boil.
Add langostinos and cook for 2 minutes. Do not overcook. Remove
immediately and chill in an ice bath.

EGGPLANT PUREE
Rub eggplant with garlic and olive oil.   Place skin down on a lightly
greased baking pan and roast until cooked, about 20 minutes. Scoop
out the flesh from the eggplant and transfer to a food processor. Add
salt and pepper, to taste, Parmigiano-Reggiano and 2 tablespoons
lemon juice. Puree until smooth.

ROOT VEGETABLE CHIPS
Peel the skin of the sweet potato, lotus root and watermelon radish and
slice paper-thin. Heat the canola oil in a very large, deep pot or heat
an electric fryer to 360 degrees F. Fry the sliced root chips, in batches,
until crisp, about 1-1/2 minutes. Drain on paper towels.

HOLLANDAISE SAUCE
In the top of double boiler set over a pot of simmering water, whisk
the egg yolks, 2 tablespoons lemon juice and Worcestershire until
smooth. Whisking vigorously, add the butter, 1 cup at a time, until all
is incorporated. Season with salt and pepper, to taste.

CREATE YOUR PLATE
Create three layers on plate. Ladle hollandaise sauce first, topped with
eggplant puree. Place 1 root vegetable chip on the puree, followed by 1
langostino. Repeat 2 more times.

Chef's Tip:

*Substitute root
vegetables
with colored
vegetable
crisps avail-
able at your
local market.*

BAKED SNAILS WITH CREAMED SPINACH

SERVES SIX

*Note: This recipe needs to be planned one day ahead.

36 snails, canned
1 bottle white wine chardonnay, reserving ½ cup
2 cups plus 2 tablespoons softened butter, divided
½ cup minced garlic, plus 2 tablespoons, divided
½ cup fresh parsley, finely chopped
½ cup fresh tarragon, finely chopped
½ cup fresh rosemary, finely chopped
1/2 tablespoon fresh oregano, finely chopped
3 tablespoons sherry wine vinegar
Sea salt
White pepper
3 cups fresh spinach
3 cups heavy cream
36 fresh white button mushrooms, stems removed
6 oven-safe ramekins
1 whole tomato, finely diced

SNAILS
Rinse snails under cold running water, then transfer to a large bowl and cover with white wine. Cover snails with a heavy plate to keep them submerged and allow them to purge overnight. Strain snails and set aside.

COMPOUND BUTTER
Place 2 cups of butter in a large bowl. Add ½ cup garlic, herbs, sherry wine vinegar and salt and pepper, to taste. Mix well. Refrigerate to harden, about 4 hours.

SNAILS WITH SPINACH AND CREAM
In a medium-size pan over moderate heat, sauté 2 tablespoons garlic and 2 tablespoons butter. Add snails and ½ cup white wine chardonnay. Simmer for approximately 3 minutes. Add spinach and cream. Simmer until the mixture reduces by one-half.

CREATE YOUR PLATE
Spoon out a small portion of spinach only from the cooked mixture and spread inside ramekin. Arrange 6 mushroom caps on top of the spinach. Insert 1 snail in each individual mushroom cap. Thinly slice compound butter and place one layer on top of snails. Repeat for each ramekin. Place 6 ramekins in oven and broil until golden brown. Once removed from oven, garnish with diced tomatoes.

Chef's Tip:

Make sure you don't over-broil the snails.

Fresh Mozzarella and Colored Peppers

Serves Six

2 pounds fresh mozzarella
1 large jar (whole) red, green and yellow peppers, more if needed
12 tablespoons basil oil
3 cups fresh basil
Sea salt
White pepper

Chef's Tip:

Use a cookie cutter to cut the mozzarella and peppers. Make sure everything is the same size so it stacks neatly.

MOZZARELLA AND PEPPERS
Cut mozzarella into 18 four inch circles. Cut peppers into 18 four inch circles

BASIL OIL SAUCE
In a blender, puree oil and basil until very smooth. Strain the mixture through a sieve back into a bowl and season with salt and pepper, to taste.

CREATE YOUR PLATE
Create three layers on each plate. Drizzle basil sauce onto the center of a plate. Place a pepper circle on top of the sauce followed by a mozzarella round. Repeat 2 times alternating the different colors of the peppers.

46

Spring Pea SOUP

CHILLED Mango Soup

Thai Coconut SOUP WITH CHICKEN

Chilled Melon SOUP

Fish Ball SOUP

Tortilla SOUP

French Onion SOUP

FIRE ROASTED Red Bell Pepper SOUP

Japanese Pumpkin SOUP

RED HEIRLOOM Tomato Gazpacho

Spring Pea Soup

SERVES SIX

2 tablespoons unsalted butter
12 cups fresh or frozen peas
1 white onion, roughly chopped
1 celery stalk, finely minced
2 cups chicken broth
3 sprigs fresh thyme, finely minced
Sea salt
White pepper
1 carrot, finely julienned
½ cup crème fraîche

Chef's Tips:

Stirring this soup constantly will prevent it from burning and sticking to the bottom of the saucepan.

You'll need a blender to puree the soup. A food processor doesn't make it smooth enough.

SPRING PEA SOUP

Heat the butter in a large saucepan over moderate heat. Add the peas, onions and celery. Stirring often, cook until the vegetables soften, about 8 minutes. Add the chicken broth and bring to a slow simmer. Add the thyme and season with salt and pepper, to taste. Adjust the heat to maintain a gentle simmer and cook, stirring constantly, until desired consistency, about 15 to 20 minutes. Watch out for hot splatters. Cool to room temperature. Transfer the soup in small batches to a blender and puree until very smooth. When ready to serve, reheat in a large saucepan by bringing to a slow simmer.

CREATE YOUR PLATE

Ladle soup into a bowl. Garnish with a small amount of julienned carrots and a light drizzle of crème fraîche.

CHILLED MANGO SOUP

12 mangos, peeled and cut into chunks
2 whole shallots, finely diced
1 cup white wine, Riesling
2 tablespoons fresh lime juice
1 pint fresh raspberries, cleaned
¼ cup granulated sugar

MANGO SOUP

In a large sauté pan, over moderate heat, sauté mangos, shallots, Riesling and lime juice until softened, about 10 minutes. Cool to room temperature. Transfer to a blender and puree until smooth. Transfer to a large bowl and cover with plastic wrap. Chill for 4 hours.

RASPBERRY COULIS

In a small saucepan, over moderate heat, sauté raspberries and sugar until the mixture resembles the consistency of jam.

CREATE YOUR PLATE

Ladle soup into a bowl. Garnish with raspberry coulis.

Chef's Tip:

You can substitute raspberry coulis for a store-bought raspberry sauce.

THAI COCONUT SOUP
WITH CHICKEN

SERVES SIX

6 cups chicken broth
2 small galanga roots, peeled and thinly sliced
2 lemongrass stalks, cut into 1-inch pieces and crushed
1-3 inch piece fresh ginger, peeled and thinly sliced
9 fresh kaffir lime leaves, torn in 1/2
1 pound boneless, skinless chicken breast, cut into thin strips
1-8 ounce can straw mushrooms, rinsed and drained
4 tablespoons Thai nam pla, or Vietnamese nuoc nam (fish sauce)
4 tablespoons palm sugar
2-13-ounce cans unsweetened coconut milk
3 limes, juiced
Sea salt
White pepper

Chef's Tip:

No need to reduce this soup; it's meant to have a thick and creamy texture.

THAI COCONUT SOUP WITH CHICKEN
In a large saucepan, combine chicken broth, galangal roots, lemongrass, ginger and kaffir lime leaves. Bring to a slow boil, then lower heat, cover, and simmer for 10 minutes to infuse the broth with flavor. Add chicken strips, mushrooms, fish sauce, sugar, coconut milk, and lime juice. Simmer until the chicken is cooked through, about 10 minutes. Season the soup with salt and pepper, to taste. Serve immediately. *Note: be careful to avoid chewing the galanga, lemongrass, ginger, or lime leaves.

CREATE YOUR PLATE
Ladle the soup into a large soup tureen or individual soup bowls.

Chilled Melon Soup

SERVES SIX

½ cantaloupe, peeled and seeded
½ medium-size watermelon, peeled and seeded
6 sprigs of fresh mint

MELON SOUP

Cut the cantaloupe and watermelon into chunks. In a large sauce-pan, over medium-high heat, sauté the melon until softened, about 10 minutes. Transfer ingredients, in small batches, to a blender and puree until smooth. Transfer to a large bowl. Cover with plastic wrap and refrigerate until chilled, about 4 hours.

CREATE YOUR PLATE

Ladle soup into a bowl. Garnish with 1 sprig of mint.

FISH BALL SOUP

SERVES SIX

24 fish balls (available at most specialty seafood markets)
1-14 ounce package firm tofu, cut into 24 slices
1 pound chicken breast, minced
6 cups chicken broth
2 cups glass noodles
2 tablespoons plus 3 teaspoons soy sauce, divided

FISH BALL SOUP
In a large saucepan, combine fish balls, tofu, chicken, chicken broth, glass noodles and 2 tablespoons soy sauce. Bring to a boil, then reduce to a slow simmer until the chicken is cooked, about 10 to 15 minutes.

CREATE YOUR PLATE
Ladle soup into a bowl. Garnish each bowl with ½ teaspoon of soy sauce.

Chef's Tip:

Serve with steamed white rice.

TORTILLA SOUP

SERVES SIX

3-14.5 ounce cans diced tomatoes
1-6 ounce can tomato paste
2 jalapenos, finely chopped
2 yellow onions, finely chopped
2 carrots, roughly chopped
3 celery stalks, roughly chopped
2 garlic cloves, roughly chopped
8 cups chicken broth
1 bag tortilla chips
1 small bunch cilantro
1 rotisserie chicken, diced or shredded

Chef's Tip:

*For added col-
or and flavor,
garnish with
colored tortilla
chips available
at your local
market.*

TORTILLA SOUP

In a large saucepan, combine tomatoes, tomato paste, jalapenos, onions, carrots, celery and garlic. Bring to a slow boil and cook until the vegetables are tender, about 15 minutes. Add chicken broth, tortilla chips and cilantro. Simmer until the liquid is reduce by one-half, about 15 minutes. Cool to room temperature. Transfer to a blender, in small batches, and puree until smooth. Place the soup back into the saucepan and heat until warm.

CREATE YOUR PLATE

Ladle soup into a bowl. Garnish with diced or shredded chicken.

FRENCH ONION SOUP

SERVES SIX

4 tablespoons olive oil
8 yellow onions, finely sliced
1 cup red wine
1 cup port wine
3 cups beef broth
Sea salt
White pepper
6 slices white bread, toasted
1 cup Gruyère cheese, shredded
6 tablespoons brandy

FRENCH ONION SOUP
In a large saucepan, heat the olive oil over medium-high heat. Add
the onions and cook, stirring constantly, until the onions are caramelized. Slowly add in the wines and simmer until the liquid is reduced by one-half. Add beef broth and continue to simmer until the
liquid is reduced by one-half. Season with salt and pepper, to taste.

BREAD SQUARES TOPPED WITH CHEESE
Heat oven to broil. Trimming off the outer crust, cut a small square
out of each bread slice. Evenly divide the cheese and place on top of
individual bread squares. Place bread squares on a baking sheet and
broil until the cheese is melted, about 1 to 2 minutes.

CREATE YOUR PLATE
Place 1 tablespoon of brandy into a small, deep soup bowl. Ladle
the soup into the bowl. Top with 1 bread square. Repeat for remaining 5 soup bowls.

Chef's Tip:

*Substitute any
cheese of your
choice.*

Fire Roasted Red Bell Pepper Soup

Serves Six

11 red bell peppers, divided
1 yellow bell pepper
3 garlic cloves, roughly chopped
6 whole shallots, roughly chopped
½ cup tomato paste
1 cup white wine, chardonnay
4 cups chicken broth
Sea salt
White pepper

ROASTED BELL PEPPERS

Preheat oven to 425 degrees F. Cover a heavy baking sheet with foil and coat with cooking spray. Arrange peppers on baking sheet and bake until the skins brown and blister, turning the peppers over occasionally, about 20 to 25 minutes. Place peppers in a bowl, cover with plastic wrap and allow to cool; about 10 minutes. Peel, seed and cut peppers into strips. *Note: reserve 1 roasted red pepper and 1 roasted yellow pepper (finely julienned) for garnish.

Chef's Tip:

This soup can be served hot or cold.

SOUP

In a large saucepan, over moderate heat, simmer the peppers, garlic, shallots and tomato paste, about 5 minutes. Slowly pour in the white wine and chicken broth. Adjust the heat to maintain a gentle simmer, and cook, stirring constantly, until desired consistency, about 30 minutes. Watch out for hot splatters. Cool to room temperature. Transfer the soup, in small batches, to a blender and puree until very smooth. When ready to serve, reheat in a large saucepan by bringing to a slow simmer. Season the soup with salt and pepper, to taste.

CREATE YOUR PLATE

Ladle soup into a bowl. Garnish with a small amount of the roasted and julienned red and yellow bell peppers.

JAPANESE PUMPKIN SOUP

SERVES SIX

6 Kabocha squash (Japanese pumpkins)
4 tablespoons olive oil
3 tablespoons honey
Sea salt
White pepper
6 garlic cloves, roughly chopped
2 yellow onions, roughly chopped
12 cups chicken broth
1 cup Gruyère cheese, shredded

Preheat oven to 450 degrees F.

PUMPKINS

Slice the top off of each pumpkin shell. Rub the inside and the out-side of the pumpkin shell with olive oil, honey and a light dusting of salt and pepper. Wrap each individual pumpkin, with its lid, in foil. Place pumpkins in the oven and bake for about 45 minutes to 1 hour. Remove from oven and cool; enough to handle. Scoop out all the pumpkin flesh from each shell. Place the pumpkin flesh in a large bowl and carefully remove as many seeds as possible.

SOUP

In a large saucepan, sauté garlic, onions and pumpkin flesh over moderate heat until caramelized, about 6 minutes. Pour in the chicken broth and simmer until the liquid is reduced by one-half, about 30 minutes. Cool. Transfer the soup, in small batches, to a blender and puree until very smooth. Strain the mixture through a sieve back into a large bowl and season with salt and pepper, to taste.

Ladle the soup into the hollow pumpkin shells and top with a pinch of shredded Gruyère cheese. Place filled pumpkins, without lids, on a large baking sheet. Place back into the oven to warm the soup and melt the cheese, about 5 minutes.

CREATE YOUR PLATE

Place pumpkin shell, filled with soup, on an individual plate with the lid on top.

Chef's Tip:

Don't worry if you can't remove every single seed from the pumpkin flesh. The blender will puree everything!

Red Heirloom Tomato Gazpacho

SERVES SIX

*Note: prepare vegetable mixture one day ahead of time.

1 red bell pepper
1 yellow bell pepper
1 green bell pepper
3 cucumbers, peeled
4 red heirloom tomatoes
1 large white onion
1 cup basil leaves
3 cups tomato juice
3 tablespoons balsamic vinegar
Sea salt
White pepper
1 lemon, juiced
2 tablespoons tomato paste
4 tablespoons extra-virgin olive oil, divided
6 shrimps (size 13/15, cleaned, peeled and deveined)
6 small rosemary stems

VEGETABLE MIXTURE
Roughly chop the peppers, cucumbers, tomatoes, onions and basil leaves and place in a large bowl. Add tomato juice, balsamic vinegar and season with salt and pepper, to taste. Mix well to combine. Cover with plastic wrap and refrigerate overnight.

Chef's Tip:

Pour the soup into pre-chilled soup bowls for an even cooler and refreshing taste.

SOUP
Transfer vegetable mixture, in small batches, to a blender and puree until very smooth. Place pureed soup in a large bowl and whisk in lemon juice, tomato paste and 2 tablespoons of olive oil. Cover with plastic wrap and refrigerate until ready to serve. Serve cold.

GRILLED SHRIMP
Preheat griddle or grill pan over high heat. Brush shrimps with 2 tablespoons of olive oil; season with salt and pepper, to taste. Grill until shrimp are opaque, about 2 minutes on each side. Thread 1 shrimp onto each rosemary skewer so that the shrimp lie flat.

CREATE YOUR PLATE
Ladle soup into a bowl. Garnish with 1 shrimp-rosemary skewer.

salads
&
vegetables

Royce SALAD

CHINESE Chicken Salad

Lobster Salad WITH ORANGE PEPPER SAUCE

Spinach SALAD

Belgian Endive Salad WITH RASPBERRY VINAIGRETTE

Curried Cous Cous AND PORTOBELLO MUSHROOM

CHORIZO Sausage Salad

CHICKEN AND Mango Salad

RADICCHIO AND Arugula Salad

TRIO OF Tomatoes

ROYCE SALAD

SERVES SIX

This infamous "Royce Salad" is an original recipe developed by **Stephen Wheeler Royce.** *It has been the most popular salad at The Inn for the last fifty years.*

½ cup mayonnaise
½ cup buttermilk
1 tablespoon yellow onion, finely minced
2 green onions, finely chopped
2 garlic cloves, crushed
4 tablespoons Italian parsley, finely chopped
1 tablespoon Worcestershire sauce
3 drops Tabasco sauce (optional)
Sea salt
White pepper
6 cups red leaf lettuce, roughly chopped
½ cup bacon pieces or bacon bits
2 avocados cut into 18 slices (3 per plate)
4 tablespoons Parmigiano-Reggiano shavings

INN RANCH DRESSING
In a large bowl combine mayonnaise, buttermilk, yellow onion, green onions, garlic, parsley, Worcestershire, Tabasco and salt and pepper, to taste. Whisk well.

ROYCE SALAD
In a large salad bowl combine lettuce with desired amount of ranch dressing. Add bacon pieces and toss gently.

CREATE YOUR PLATE
Place salad onto a plate. Top with 3 avocado slices and garnish with shaved Parmigiano-Reggiano.

Chef's Tip:

Once dressed, serve this salad immediately to keep the lettuce from wilting.

CHINESE CHICKEN SALAD

SERVES SIX

6 boneless, skinless, chicken breasts, about 6 ounces each
2 tablespoons extra virgin olive oil
Sea salt
White pepper
1 cup peanut butter
2 cups heavy cream
2 tablespoons sesame oil
3 Thai chilies, diced
1 cup raw peanuts, unsalted
6 cups red cabbage, shredded
6 cups green cabbage, shredded
1 each red, yellow and green pepper, julienned
2 cups rice noodles

CHICKEN BREASTS
Spray a grill or grill pan with cooking spray and heat to medium-high heat. Rub chicken breasts with olive oil and season with salt and pepper, to taste. Grill until grill marks have formed and chicken is cooked through, about 5 minutes per side. Slice the breasts into thin strips.

PEANUT DRESSING
In a large non-stick saucepan, over moderate heat, combine peanut butter, heavy cream, sesame oil and chilies. Whisking constantly, cook until smooth, about 5 to 6 minutes. Remove from heat. Add peanuts. Mix well.

CHINESE CHICKEN SALAD
In a large bowl, combine chicken, cabbage, peppers, and rice noodles. Drizzle with peanut dressing and toss to coat.

CREATE YOUR PLATE
Place salad into a large salad bowl and serve family style.

Lobster Salad with Orange Pepper Sauce

SERVES SIX

4 lobster tails cooked, about 1 pound each
1 red bell pepper
1 green bell pepper
3 orange bell peppers, divided
1 celery stick
½ of a large red onion
½ cup mayonnaise
½ cup lemon juice
2 teaspoons fresh tarragon, finely minced
Sea salt
White pepper
1 cup fresh squeezed orange juice

LOBSTER SALAD
Mince the lobster, red pepper, green pepper, 1 orange pepper, celery and onions. Place in a large mixing bowl. Add mayonnaise, lemon juice, tarragon and salt and pepper, to taste. Mix well.

ORANGE PEPPER SAUCE
In a saucepan over medium-high heat, simmer 2 orange peppers (finely minced) with the orange juice until the peppers are soft, about 15 minutes. Remove from heat and cool to room temperature. Transfer mixture to a blender and puree until smooth. Strain the sauce through a sieve into a large bowl and season with salt and pepper, to taste.

CREATE YOUR PLATE
Spoon the lobster salad onto the center of a plate. Drizzle orange pepper sauce around the lobster salad.

Chef's Tip:

Garnish with fresh avocado chunks stuffed with fresh lobster meat or fresh lemon wedges.

SPINACH SALAD

SERVES SIX

1 cup honey
2 tablespoons balsamic vinegar
3 tablespoons Dijon mustard
½ cup extra virgin olive oil
1 lemon, juiced
Sea salt
White pepper
6 cups baby spinach
1 cup Stilton cheese
1 cup corn
1 cup bacon pieces or bacon bits
6 large eggs, cooked to desired liking

Chef's Tip:

Pour dressing over the salad when ready to serve to prevent the spinach leaves from wilting.

HONEY-MUSTARD DRESSING
In a large bowl, combine honey, vinegar, mustard, olive oil, lemon and salt and pepper, to taste.

SPINACH SALAD
In a large bowl, combine baby spinach with Stilton cheese, corn and bacon pieces. Drizzle with honey-mustard dressing. Toss gently.

CREATE YOUR PLATE
Portion salad onto a plate. Place egg on top.

Belgian Endive Salad with Raspberry Vinaigrette

SERVES SIX

3 pints fresh raspberries, divided
5 tablespoons raspberry vinegar
10 tablespoons vegetable oil
3 tablespoons granulated sugar
3 shallots, minced
3 sprigs of fresh thyme
Sea salt
White pepper
2 large red Belgian endives
2 large yellow Belgian endives
1 cup blue cheese, crumbled
18 candied walnuts

RASPBERRY VINAIGRETTE
In a large bowl, finely crush 2 pints of raspberries with a fork. Slowly whisk in vinegar, vegetable oil, sugar, shallots, thyme and a pinch of salt and pepper.

SALAD
Cut 1/4-inch from the bottom of the endives and peel away the outer leaves. (Reserve the inner core for another use). In a large bowl, combine the endive leaves with the blue cheese, walnuts and 1 pint of whole fresh raspberries. Gently toss the salad with enough raspberry vinaigrette to coat. Season the salad with salt and pepper, to taste.

CREATE YOUR PLATE
Portion salad onto 6 salad plates.

Chef's Tip:

For an extra splash of flavor and color, drizzle any remaining vinaigrette on individual salads.

CURRIED COUS COUS AND PORTOBELLO MUSHROOM

SERVES SIX

2 cups plain cooked couscous
2 tablespoons curry powder
1 whole cauliflower
4 cups chicken broth
1 tablespoons butter
2 teaspoons garlic, roughly chopped, divided
½ yellow onion, roughly chopped
1/2 cup heavy cream
6 large Portobello mushrooms
3 tablespoons extra-virgin olive oil, divided
4 cups fresh or frozen green peas
3 cups vegetable broth
3 cups fresh baby spinach
6 (1-cup) bottomless molds

COUS COUS
Cook the cous cous according to package directions and set aside, covered to keep warm. *Note: season cous cous with curry powder.

CAULIFLOWER PUREE
Rinse cauliflower. Cut off the stem and trim into florets. In a large saucepan, combine the cauliflower and chicken broth. Bring to a boil, then reduce heat to a slow simmer and cook the cauliflower until soft. Remove from heat and drain. In a small sauté pan, over moderate heat, sauté butter, 1 teaspoon of garlic and onions. Cook until slightly tender. Transfer the cauliflower with butter, garlic and onion mixture to a food processor. Add the cream and puree until smooth. Season with salt and pepper, to taste.

PORTOBELLO MUSHROOM
Rub mushrooms with 2 tablespoons of olive oil and salt and pepper, to taste. On a grill pan or outdoor grill, cook the mushrooms until tender, about 3 minutes on each side. Cool to the touch and cut into circles, about 4 inches in diameter.

GREEN PEA PUREE
In a large saucepan, combine peas and vegetable broth. Bring to a slow boil. Reduce heat to slow simmer and cook the peas until tender. Cool to room temperature. Transfer to a blender and puree until smooth.

SAUTEED SPINACH

In a skillet, heat 1 tablespoon of olive oil and 1 teaspoon of garlic over moderate heat. Cook until just fragrant. Add spinach and sauté until cooked, but still tender. Drain. Add salt and pepper, to taste.

CREATE YOUR PLATE

Spoon some green pea puree onto the bottom of a plate. Center 1 mold on top of the puree and fill with ingredients, 1 layer at a time. Start with the cous cous, followed by the cauliflower puree and ending with the mushroom. Gently lift the mold. Garnish with spinach.

Chorizo Sausage Salad

SERVES SIX

12 small red potatoes, peeled
1/2 cup mayonnaise, divided
2 tablespoons crushed garlic, divided
Sea salt
White pepper
1 tablespoon capers
18 thick slices chorizo sausage
3 cups mixed greens
1 tablespoon extra virgin olive oil
1 teaspoon lemon juice
18 anchovies

POTATOES

Place potatoes in a large pot. Bring to a boil, reduce heat to simmer and cook until tender, about 10 minutes. Place in a large bowl of ice water. Drain. Cut potatoes into slices and place in a large bowl. Add ¼ cup of mayonnaise and 1 tablespoons of garlic. Season with salt and pepper, to taste. Toss lightly to coat.

GARLIC MAYONNAISE

In a small bowl, combine ¼ cup of mayonnaise with 1 tablespoon of garlic and capers. Whisk well.

GRILLED CHORIZO SAUSAGE

Heat an outdoor grill or grill pan to high heat. Grill sausage until done, about 2 minutes on each side.

MIXED GREEN SALAD

Place mixed greens in a large bowl. Drizzle with olive oil and lemon juice. Season with salt and pepper, to taste. Lightly toss.

CREATE YOUR PLATE

Spread garlic mayonnaise onto a plate with potato salad on top. Arrange 3 sausage slices and 3 anchovies around the plate. Garnish with mixed green salad.

Chef's Tip:

Clean and leave the skin on the potatoes if you like.

Chicken and Mango Salad

Serves Six

2 boneless, skinless, chicken breasts, about 6 ounces each
1 teaspoon extra virgin olive oil
Sea salt
White pepper
3 large mangos
½ cup green onions, finely chopped
2 celery stalks, finely chopped
1 each red, yellow and green bell pepper, finely chopped, reserve some for garnish
½ cup mayonnaise
½ teaspoon garlic powder
Sea salt
White pepper
1 cup banana chips

CHICKEN BREASTS
Spray a grill or grill pan with cooking spray and heat to medium-high heat. Rub chicken breasts with olive oil and season with salt and pepper, to taste. Grill until grill marks have formed and chicken is cooked through, about 5 minutes per side. Slice the breasts into small chunks.

MANGOS
Peel and cut the mangos in half. *Note- you will need ½ mango per plate.

CHICKEN SALAD
In a large bowl, combine chicken, onions, celery, peppers, mayonnaise, garlic, and salt and pepper, to taste.

CREATE YOUR PLATE
Place mango on the center of a plate. Fill with chicken salad. Garnish with finely chopped colored peppers around the plate and banana chips on top.

Chef's Tip:

Garnish with banana chips available at your local market.

Radicchio and Arugula Salad

Serves Six

3 shallots, minced
½ cup balsamic vinegar
½ cup extra-virgin olive oil
Sea salt
White pepper
3 fresh red radicchio heads, roughly chopped
3 cups fresh baby arugula, left whole
3 tablespoons Parmigiano-Reggiano shavings, more if desired

BALSAMIC VINAIGRETTE
In a bowl, combine shallots, balsamic, olive oil, and salt and pepper, to taste. Whisk well.

SALAD
In a large bowl combine radicchio and arugula. Slowly add desired amount of vinaigrette to the radicchio and arugula salad. Toss gently and serve immediately.

CREATE YOUR PLATE
Place salad onto a plate and garnish with Parmigiano-Reggiano shavings.

TRIO OF TOMATOES

SERVES SIX

2 large red beefsteak tomatoes, halved and quartered
2 large green beefsteak tomatoes, halved and quartered
2 large orange or yellow beefsteak tomatoes, halved and quartered
1 cup fresh basil
1 garlic clove
¼ cup, plus 3 tablespoons extra virgin olive oil, divided
3 tablespoons grated parmesan cheese
1 tablespoon pine nuts
Sea salt
White pepper
1 cup blue cheese dressing
½ cup balsamic vinegar
½ teaspoon fresh Italian oregano, finely chopped

PESTO
In a blender, puree basil, garlic, ¼ cup olive oil, and parmesan cheese. Transfer to a small bowl. Stir in pine nuts and season with salt and pepper, to taste.

BALSAMIC VINAIGRETTE
In a small bowl combine balsamic vinegar, 3 tablespoons olive oil, oregano and salt and pepper, to taste. Whisk well.

CREATE YOUR PLATE
In separate portions, ladle a spoonful of the pesto, blue cheese dressing and balsamic vinaigrette onto a rectangular plate. Place 1 red tomato quarter on top of pesto, 1 green tomato quarter on top of blue cheese dressing and 1 orange tomato quarter on top of balsamic vinaigrette.

seafood

Tandoori Prawns WITH COCONUT SAUCE

LOBSTER Tomato Termidor

Grilled Swordfish WITH LOBSTER SAUCE

Lobster with Morel AND CHANTERELLE SAUCE

Soft-Shell Crab WITH THAI MANGO SALAD

Grilled Tuna WITH VEGETABLES

Dover Sole WITH CUCUMBER SAUCE

Steamed Halibut WITH BOK CHOY

SEAFOOD Vongole

Scallop Flower WITH GOLDEN CAVIAR

Sea Bass WITH RICE NOODLES

SHRIMP Fried Rice

Fettuccini WITH TIGER PRAWNS

GRILLED John Dory

Wok Fried Lobster IN THAI CHILI SAUCE

Alaskan King Salmon IN RED WINE BEURRE BLANC SAUCE

WRAPPED Codfish IN PASSION FRUIT SAUCE

Sundried Tomato CRUSTED HALIBUT

PAN ROASTED Chilean Sea Bass

TANDOORI PRAWNS WITH COCONUT SAUCE

SERVES SIX

6 cups chicken broth, divided
1 cup basmati rice
2 red bell peppers, roughly chopped
2 yellow bell peppers, roughly chopped
1 yellow onion, finely chopped
Sea salt
White pepper
3 cups unsweetened coconut milk
¼ cup cornstarch
18 jumbo prawns (size 4-6 count, shelled and deveined)
1 cup tandoori paste
½ cup plain yogurt
2 tablespoons fresh ginger, chopped
2 tablespoons fresh lemongrass, chopped
6 metal or wooden skewers that have been soaked

RICE
In a large saucepan, bring 3 cups chicken broth to a boil.   Add rice.
Simmer until rice is tender, about 20 minutes.

BELL PEPPER SAUCE
In a large saucepan combine peppers, onions and 3 cups chicken
broth. Bring to a boil, then reduce heat to a slow simmer and cook
until the peppers are soft, about 15 minutes. Transfer ingredients to
a blender and puree until smooth. Strain through a sieve into a large
bowl. Season with salt and pepper, to taste.

COCONUT SAUCE
In a large non-stick saucepan, bring the coconut milk to a slow boil.
Slowly add in cornstarch, a little at a time, whisking constantly, until
the mixture is thick and creamy. Remove from heat and cool.

PRAWNS
In a large skillet, over medium-high heat, simmer prawns, tandoori
paste, ½ cup yogurt, ginger and lemon grass until the prawns are
cooked, about 6 minutes. Thread 3 shrimp each per skewer.

CREATE YOUR PLATE
Ladle bell pepper sauce onto the bottom of a plate. Portion rice on
top of the sauce. Position shrimp skewer on the rice. Drizzle coconut sauce over the shrimp.

Chef's Tip:

*A good rule to
remember is 3
cups of chicken
broth to 1 cup
of rice.*

Lobster Tomato Termidor

SERVES SIX

12 cups water
Sea salt
White pepper
6 cups wild rice
6-1 pound lobster tails
6 tablespoons extra virgin olive oil, divided
1 cup chopped garlic
1 cup shallots, finely diced, divided
2 cups fresh basil leaves
2 teaspoons unsalted butter
2 cups heavy cream
2 cups white wine
3 cups tomatoes, diced
2 cups grated Parmigiano-Reggiano
1 bottle red wine, merlot
3 cups butter

WILD RICE
In a large pot, bring 12 cups of water and 3 teaspoons of salt to a boil. Add the rice and stir well. Reduce the heat to low, cover, and simmer for 45 minutes to 1 hour. Drain excess liquid from the rice.

LOBSTER

Chef's Tip:

Before adding the cooked lobster mixture back into its shell, make sure it isn't runny.

Cut lobster shells gently back and scoop out lobster meat and set aside. Chop lobster meat coarsely. In a large sauté pan, over medium-high heat, sauté 3 tablespoons olive oil, garlic and ½ cup shallots. Add lobster meat, basil leaves, butter, cream, white wine, tomatoes, and salt and pepper, to taste. Simmer over moderate heat until done, about 10 minutes. When most of the liquid has been reduced and absorbed, add the Parmigiano-Reggiano. Fill hollow lobster shells with cooked mixture. Place the lobster shells on a broiler pan and broil in the oven until topping becomes golden brown, about 2 minutes.

RED WINE BEURRE BLANC SAUCE
In a medium-size, heavy saucepan, heat 3 tablespoons of olive oil over medium-high heat. Add 1/2 cup shallots and sauté until tender, about 10 minutes. Slowly stir in red wine. Reduce heat and simmer uncovered, stirring often, until the mixture reduces by one-half, about 30 minutes. Cover sauce and cool to room temperature. Whisk in of butter 1 cup at a time, stirring constantly until creamy.

CREATE YOUR PLATE
Spoon wild rice onto a plate with lobster tail on top. Drizzle beurre blanc sauce around the plate.

GRILLED SWORDFISH WITH LOBSTER SAUCE

3 cups lobster broth
1 cup brandy
6 swordfish fillets, about 6 ounces each
5 tablespoons extra-virgin olive oil, divided
Sea salt
White pepper
2 (10-ounce) packages of spring salad mix

LOBSTER SAUCE
In a large bowl, combine lobster broth and brandy. Mix well.

SWORDFISH
Preheat a stovetop grill to medium-high. Brush both sides of the
swordfish fillets with 3 tablespoons olive oil and season with salt
and pepper, to taste.   Grill the fish until cooked through, about 4 to
5 minutes per side. Remove from the grill and cover with foil to keep
warm.

SPRING MIX
In a large bowl, toss spring mix with 2 tablespoons olive oil and
season with salt and pepper, to taste.

CREATE YOUR PLATE
Spoon lobster sauce onto a plate with spring mix on top. Place
swordfish on top of the spring mix.

Lobster with Morel and Chanterelle Cream Sauce

SERVES SIX

2 tablespoons peppercorns
3 bay leaves
1 lemon, juiced
6 lobster tails, about 6 ounces each
1 tablespoon garlic, minced
4 tablespoons extra-virgin olive oil, divided
3 cups fresh spinach
White wine, a splash
1 cup morel mushrooms
1 cup chanterelle mushrooms
2 cups heavy cream
Sea salt
White pepper

LOBSTER
Fill a large saucepan with water; enough to immerse 6 lobster tails.
Add peppercorns, bay leaves and lemon juice to the water. Bring to
a boil and carefully drop in lobster tails. Boil until the lobster tails
are cooked, about 4 to 6 minutes. Remove lobster tails from the
water and refrigerate until cold, about an hour. When ready to serve,
gently cut back the lobster shell and remove the meat. Cut the meat
of each tail into 3 pieces.

SPINACH
In a large sauté pan, over moderate heat, sauté garlic in 2 tablespoons of olive oil until fragrant. Add spinach and a splash of white
wine. Stirring often, cook the spinach until tender, about 5 to 8
minutes.

MOREL AND CHANTERELLE CREAM SAUCE
In a large sauté pan, over medium high heat, sauté mushrooms in 2
tablespoons of olive oil. Stirring often, cook until the mushrooms
are tender, about 5 to 10 minutes. Add 2 cups of heavy cream and
reduce heat to a slow simmer until the cream is reduced by one-half.
Season with salt and pepper, to taste. Transfer mixture to a blender
and puree until smooth. When ready to serve, transfer mixture to a
saucepan, and warm over low-moderate heat. Add the lobster meat
to the cream sauce if you prefer the lobster warm. *Note: Be careful
not to burn the cream mixture.

CREATE YOUR PLATE
Ladle the mushroom cream sauce onto a plate. Spoon spinach on
top of the sauce. Arrange 3 pieces of lobster on top of the spinach.

Chef's Tip:

*If you want the
lobster warm,
add the meat
to the warm
mushroom
sauce before
serving.*

Soft-Shell Crab with Thai Mango Salad

SERVES SIX

Canola oil, for deep frying
6 soft-shell crabs
1 cup cornstarch, more if needed
Sea salt
White pepper
4 mangos, julienned
1 large red onion, peeled and minced
3 tablespoons fish sauce
2 limes, juiced
½ cup unsalted roasted peanuts
Thai chilies, julienned, to taste (optional)

Heat the canola oil in a very large, deep pot or heat an electric fryer to 360 degrees F.

SOFT-SHELL CRABS
Rinse and clean crabs in cold water, then pat dry with paper towels. Place cornstarch into a large bowl and season with salt and pepper, to taste. Lightly dredge each crab in the cornstarch, making sure that the crabs are completely coated. Hold crabs by long tongs, lower into the oil, and fry until golden brown, about 2 to 3 minutes. Turn crabs over and continue frying for an additional 2 to 3 minutes, or until crispy or golden brown all over. Carefully transfer crabs to drain on paper towels.

THAI MANGO SALAD
In a large bowl combine mangos, onions, fish sauce, lime juice, peanuts and chilies. Mix well.

CREATE YOUR PLATE
Layer mango salad onto a plate and top with one 1 soft-shell crab.

Chef's Tip:

If you can't find fresh mangos, use frozen mangos available at your local market.

GRILLED TUNA WITH VEGETABLES

SERVES SIX

Six tuna fillets, about 6 ounces each
5 tablespoons extra-virgin olive oil, divided
Sea salt
White pepper
1 avocado, peeled and chopped
4 shallots (two diced) (two finely chopped)
2 tablespoons fresh cilantro, finely chopped
1 lemon, juiced
2 tablespoons sesame oil
1 tablespoon white sesame seeds
1 tablespoon black sesame seeds
3 cups fresh squeezed orange juice
2 tablespoons soy sauce
3 tablespoons fresh ginger grated
1 leek, finely chopped
2 tablespoons cornstarch
1 cup granulated sugar
2 cloves garlic, finely chopped
1 red bell pepper, julienned
1 yellow bell pepper, julienned
1 green zucchini, julienned
5 shitake mushrooms, julienned
1 cup enoki mushrooms
1 cup snow peas
1 red onion, finely chopped
2 each baby bok choy, roughly chopped
6 won ton skins

TUNA
Heat an outdoor grill or non-stick stovetop grill (coated with 2 table-spoons olive oil) to medium-high heat. Season both sides of tuna fillets with salt and pepper. Grill fillets 2 to 3 minutes per side for medium doneness.

AVOCADO RELISH
In a small bowl, add avocado, diced shallots, cilantro, lemon juice, sesame oil, sesame seeds and salt and pepper, to taste. Mix well.

PONZU SAUCE
Add orange juice to a medium-size saucepan. Stir in soy sauce, ginger, leeks and finely chopped shallots and bring to a boil. Reduce heat and whisk in cornstarch to thicken. Add sugar and stir until smooth. Remove from heat. Strain and cover.

VEGETABLES
In a large wok, over moderate heat, sauté garlic in 3 tablespoons olive oil until fragrant. Add in all the vegetables, season with salt and pepper, to taste, and stir fry until tender.

CREATE YOUR PLATE
Place vegetables onto the center of a plate with tuna on top. Dollop avocado relish on top of tuna. Garnish with wonton skin. Finish by drizzling ponzu sauce around the plate.

Chef's Tip:

Make sure to cook the veggies al dente to preserve flavor and color. Substitute any vegetables you prefer.

DOVER SOLE WITH CUCUMBER SAUCE

SERVES SIX

9 Idaho potatoes
4 tablespoons butter
1 head of fennel, finely diced
1 beet root, finely diced
Sea salt
White pepper
6 Dover Sole fillets, about 6 ounces each
2 cups all purpose flour, more if needed
4 tablespoons extra-virgin olive oil
1 whole cucumber, peeled and cut into chunks
8 ounces plain yogurt
1 tablespoon lemon juice

RED POTATOES
Peel, rinse, and dice the potatoes. Dry thoroughly with a thick towel.
In a large skillet, heat the butter over medium-high heat. Add the
potatoes, fennel, beet root, and salt and pepper, to taste. Stirring
constantly, cook until the potatoes are tender and red in color, about
15 minutes.

DOVER SOLE
Season fillets with salt and pepper, to taste. Lightly dredge fillets in
flour. In a large skillet, heat the olive oil over high heat until almost
smoking. Add the fillets to the pan and cook until golden brown,
about 3 minutes per side.

CUCUMBER SAUCE
In a blender, combine cucumber, yogurt, lemon juice and salt and
pepper, to taste. Puree until smooth.

CREATE YOUR PLATE
Arrange potatoes in the center of a plate. Place fish fillet on top.
Drizzle cucumber sauce around the plate.

STEAMED HALIBUT WITH BOK CHOY

SERVES SIX

6 each baby bok choy
6 halibut fillets, about 6 ounces each
2 Thai chilies, julienned
6 tablespoons sesame oil
6 tablespoons soy sauce
18 slices of ginger root

Preheat oven to 400 degrees F.

BOK CHOY AND HALIBUT
Arrange bok choy in a large baking dish.   Layer halibut fillets on top.
Sprinkle chilies on top and drizzle with sesame oil and soy sauce.
Cover with foil and bake until fish is cooked through, about 10 to 12
minutes.

CREATE YOUR PLATE
Place 1 bok choy onto a plate followed by 1 fillet on top. Garnish
with 3 ginger slices around the plate.

Seafood Vongole

SERVES SIX

3 tablespoons extra-virgin olive oil
4 garlic cloves, minced
5 pounds fresh clams, scrubbed and rinsed (New Zealand cockles or Manila clams)
1/2 white onion, thinly sliced
1 cup dry white wine
2 cups clam juice
1 cup cilantro, roughly chopped
4 Thai chilies, roughly chopped
½ teaspoon chili powder, optional

Heat a large saucepan with olive oil over moderate heat. Add garlic and clams and toss lightly. Add the remaining ingredients. Cover and bring to a slow boil. Once the clams open, it's ready!

CREATE YOUR PLATE
Place seafood vongole in a large serving bowl and serve family style.

Chef's Tip:

Only add chili powder to this recipe if you want it spicy.

Scallop Flower with Golden Caviar

Serves Six

¼ cup plus 5 tablespoons extra-virgin olive oil, divided
1 medium white onion, finely minced
2 cups Arborio rice
3-1/2 cups port wine
Sea salt
White pepper
3 cups freshly squeezed orange juice
2 shallots, minced
2 tablespoons honey
½ cup white wine, chardonnay
1-1/2 cups butter, softened
8 Scallops (size U-10)
1 cup salmon caviar

RED WINE RISOTTO
In a large saucepan, heat 5 tablespoons olive oil over medium heat. Add the onions and cook until softened and translucent, about 8 minutes. Once the onions are translucent, add the rice and stir with a wooden spoon until toasted, about 3 to 4 minutes. Add the wine to the toasting rice, and cook, stirring constantly, until it is absorbed and the rice is al dente, about 15 minutes. Season with salt and pepper, to taste.

CITRUS GLAZE
In a large saucepan combine orange juice, shallots, honey and white wine over medium heat. Simmer until reduced by one-half, about 15 minutes. Set aside to cool for about 5 minutes, then whisk in butter until smooth.

SCALLOPS
Season scallops on both sides with salt and pepper, to taste. Slice each scallop lengthwise into three slices, for a total of 24 slices. Heat ¼ cup olive oil in a large sauté pan over medium-high heat. Place the scallops in the pan and cook until golden brown, about 15 seconds per side.

CREATE YOUR PLATE
Drizzle citrus glaze onto a plate. Portion the red wine risotto on top of the glaze. Place 4 scallops on top of the risotto. Carefully arrange caviar around the risotto.

Chef's Tip:

If you don't like red wine risotto, use 3-1/2 cups of chicken broth in place of the port wine.

SEA BASS WITH RICE NOODLES

Canola oil, for frying
2 pounds sea bass fillets cut into thick slices
Sea salt
White pepper
1 cup cornstarch, more if needed
3 tablespoons peanut oil
4 garlic cloves, crushed
½ yellow onion, sliced
1 cup bean sprouts
2 packages rice noodles
3 tablespoons oyster sauce
½ cup fish broth
1 cup brandy

Heat the canola oil in a very large, deep pot or heat an electric fryer to 360 degrees F.

DEEP-FRIED SEA BASS
Lightly season sliced fillets with salt and pepper. Add cornstarch to a large bowl. Lightly dredge fillets in the cornstarch, making sure each one is completely coated. Lower fillets into the oil and deep fry until crispy and golden brown, about 3 minutes. Carefully transfer fillets to drain on paper towels.

VEGETABLES AND RICE NOODLES
In a large wok, heat peanut oil, garlic and onions over moderate heat. Stirring constantly, add sprouts, noodles, oyster sauce, fish broth and brandy. Bring to medium-high heat and sauté all the ingredients until the noodles are cooked al dente, about 3 minutes.

CREATE YOUR PLATE
Arrange vegetables and rice noodles on a large serving platter. Place fried sea bass on top.

SHRIMP FRIED RICE

SERVES SIX

2 cups cooked jasmine rice, or long-grain white rice
7 tablespoons corn oil, divided
3 garlic cloves, finely minced
2 carrots, finely diced
2 green onions, finely chopped
2 tomatoes, finely chopped
2 eggs, beaten
2 tablespoons soy sauce
2 teaspoons sesame oil
¼ cup cilantro, finely chopped
Sea salt
White pepper
40 shrimp, (size 26-30), peeled and deveined
2 Japanese cucumbers, thinly sliced

Note: Cook the jasmine or long-grain rice according to package directions and set aside, covered to keep warm.

JASMINE RICE WITH VEGETABLES
In a large skillet or wok, heat 3 tablespoons of oil over medium-high heat. Add garlic, carrots, onions and tomatoes. Cook until just tender. Remove the vegetables and pour eggs in the pan. Scramble eggs and add the vegetables back into the pan. Add rice, soy sauce, sesame oil and cilantro. Toss gently to combine. Season with salt and pepper, to taste.

SHRIMP
In a large skillet or wok, heat 4 tablespoons of oil over medium-high heat. Add shrimp to the pan and cook until the shrimp are just cooked through, about 3 to 4 minutes.

CREATE YOUR PLATE
Decorate the edge of a large round serving platter with cucumber slices. Mold rice in a large bowl and flip upside down onto the center of the platter. Scatter shrimp on top and around the sides of the rice.

Chef's Tip:

Serve with soy sauce or dipping sauce of your choice.

FETTUCCINI WITH TIGER PRAWNS

SERVES SIX

3 cups Pernod
½ cup extra-virgin olive oil
3 garlic cloves, finely minced
½ cup parsley, finely chopped
2 red tomatoes, finely diced
1 cup kalamata olives, chopped
Sea salt
White pepper
6 tiger prawns (size U-3, with the heads and tails left on)
1 pound fresh fettuccini

PERNOD SAUCE
In a large bowl, combine Pernod, olive oil, garlic, parsley, tomatoes, kalamata olives and salt and pepper, to taste. Mix well.

TIGER SHRIMP
Cut shrimp down the back and clean. Heat a grill pan or outdoor grill to high heat. Grill the shrimp until cooked, about 3 minutes per side.

FETTUCCINI
In a large pot of salted boiling water, add fresh fettuccini and cook until al dente, about 2 minutes. Drain.

CREATE YOUR PLATE
Add the fettuccini to a large serving bowl. Pour Pernod sauce over the top. Toss gently to combine. Arrange the tiger prawns on top of the fettuccini. Serve family style.

Chef's Tips:

You can substitute 1 box (16 ounces) of store-bought fettuccini. Cook according to the package instructions.

Before adding the tiger shrimp on top, garnish the fettuccini with freshly grated Parmigiano-Reggiano.

GRILLED JOHN DORY

2 cups white wine, chardonnay
3 whole shallots, finely minced
2 cups heavy cream
2 tablespoons black caviar
Sea salt
White pepper
4 tablespoon extra-virgin olive oil, divided
3 heads baby romaine lettuce
18 purple pearl onions
18 white pearl onions
18 ears canned baby corn, drained
6 John Dory fillets, about 5 ounces each
1 cup all purpose flour, more if needed

CAVIAR CREAM SAUCE
In a large saucepan, over medium-high heat, combine the wine and shallots. Bring to a boil and cook until the wine is reduced by one-half. Reduce the heat to medium, add the cream, and simmer until thickened and reduced enough to coat the back of a spoon, about 2 to 3 minutes. Add the caviar, stir to blend, and remove from the heat. Season with salt and pepper, to taste. Cover to keep warm until ready to serve.

SAUTÉED BABY ROMAINE AND VEGETABLES
In a large sauté pan, heat 2 tablespoons olive oil over moderate heat. Add the romaine, onions and baby corn. Sauté until tender, about 5 minutes.

GRILLED JOHN DORY FILLETS
Rinse the fish fillets and pat dry. Season with salt and pepper, to taste. Lightly dust the fillets with flour on both sides. Heat a stovetop grill pan with 2 tablespoons olive oil over medium-high heat. Add fillets to the pan and cook until done, about 2 to 3 minutes on each side (be careful not to break the fillets when flipping).

CREATE YOUR PLATE
Spoon caviar cream sauce onto the center of a plate. Scatter sautéed baby romaine and vegetables on top of the sauce. Place John Dory fillet on top of the vegetables.

WOK FRIED LOBSTER IN THAI CHILI SAUCE

SERVES SIX

Canola oil, for frying
1 cup cornstarch, more if needed
Sea salt
White pepper
6 fresh or frozen lobster tails, cut into chunks
2 tablespoons peanut oil
3 tablespoons garlic, crushed
1 small yellow onion, finely sliced
2 cups sweet and sour Thai chili sauce
2 tablespoons green onion, finely chopped

Heat the canola oil in a very large, deep pot or heat an electric fryer to 360 degrees F.

Chef's Tip:

Serve lobster with seamed white rice.

LOBSTER
In a large bowl combine cornstarch and salt and pepper, to taste. Lightly dredge lobster in the cornstarch, making sure each one is completely coated. Lower lobster into the oil and deep fry until crispy, about 1 minute. Carefully transfer lobster to drain on paper towels.

GARLIC AND ONIONS
In a wok, heat peanut oil to medium-high heat. Add garlic and yellow onions. Sauté until caramelized.

LOBSTER WITH GARLIC, ONIONS AND THAI CHILI SAUCE
In a large bowl, combine lobster with caramelized garlic and onions. Add sweet and sour Thai chili sauce. Toss gently to combine.

CREATE YOUR PLATE
Place lobster onto a large platter. Garnish with green onions.

Alaskan King Salmon in Red Wine Beurre Blanc Sauce

SERVES SIX

6 king salmon fillets, about 6 ounces each
Sea salt
White pepper
6 tablespoons extra-virgin olive oil, divided
2 tablespoons crushed garlic
3 cups plus 2 tablespoons softened butter, divided
48 marbled baby potatoes, blanched and tender
3 sprigs of fresh thyme, leaves removed from stem
2 whole shallots, finely diced
1 bottle red wine, merlot
18 asparagus spears, blanched

SALMON
Preheat oven to 350 degrees F. Lightly season salmon fillets on both sides with salt and pepper. In a large skillet, heat 3 tablespoons of olive oil over medium-high heat. Add the salmon fillets and cook for about 2 minutes on each side. Transfer to a baking sheet and finish in the oven until fork tender.

POTATOES
In a large, heavy skillet, over medium-high heat, sauté crushed garlic and 2 tablespoons of butter until fragrant. Add the marbled potatoes and thyme. Toss gently to combine.

RED WINE BEURRE BLANC SAUCE
In a medium-size, heavy saucepan, heat 3 tablespoons of olive oil over medium-high heat. Add shallots and sauté until tender, about 5 to 7 minutes. Slowly stir in red wine. Reduce heat and simmer, stirring often, until the mixture reduces by one-half, about 30 minutes. Cover sauce and cool to room temperature. Whisk in 3 cups of butter, a little at a time, until creamy.

CREATE YOUR PLATE
Place salmon fillet onto the center of a plate. Strategically place 4 potatoes to the right and 4 potatoes to the left of the fillet. Drizzle beurre blanc sauce around the plate. Garnish with 3 asparagus spears.

Chef's Tip:

Before adding butter to the beurre blanc, make sure to cool the sauce to room temperature. Add the butter slowly and carefully to avoid the sauce from separating.

WRAPPED CODFISH IN PASSION FRUIT SAUCE

SERVES SIX

6 codfish fillets, about 6 ounces each
Sea salt
White pepper
6 sheets rice paper (each piece large enough to wrap a 6 ounce codfish fillet)
18 whole cilantro leaves
½ cup canola oil for frying, more if needed
1 jar roasted red and yellow bell peppers
2 teaspoons pommery mustard
3 tablespoons extra-virgin olive oil
1 lemon grass stick, finely chopped
2 cups fresh passion fruit, peeled and finely minced
2 limes, juiced
1 teaspoon cinnamon
3 jalapenos, sliced into 18 thin circles (optional garnish)

Chef's Tip:

Cook the cod on a low flame so that the fish wrapper doesn't burn.

CODFISH IN RICE PAPER
Lightly season codfish fillets on both sides with salt and pepper. Dip rice paper in cold water (this helps it soften and stick together easily). Place 3 leaves of cilantro onto 1 rice paper square. Place 1 codfish fillet on top of cilantro and wrap tightly (you should see the cilantro leaves through the rice paper). Repeat process for remaining 5 rice paper sheets. In a large sauté pan, fry the wrapped-codfish in canola oil over medium-low heat until golden brown, about 3 minutes per side.

PEPPER POMMERY MARMALADE
Remove 3 red peppers and 3 yellow peppers from the jar and slice into thin strips. Combine peppers, mustard and olive oil in a small saucepan. Simmer over medium heat until warm, about 1 minute. Remove from heat. Add lemon grass and mix well.

PASSION FRUIT SAUCE
In a large bowl, combine passion fruit, lime juice and cinnamon. Mix well.

CREATE YOUR PLATE

Spoon pepper pommery marmalade onto the center of a plate. Arrange a cod fillet on top of the marmalade. Drizzle passion fruit sauce around the fish. Garnish with 3 sliced jalapeno circles.

Sundried Tomato Crusted Halibut

SERVES SIX

5 tablespoons extra-virgin olive oil, divided
6 halibut fillets, about 6 ounces each
Sea salt
White pepper
2 cups sundried tomatoes in oil
2 cups Italian bread crumbs
6 medium-sized yellow heirloom tomatoes, cored
2 shallots, roughly chopped
1 celery stick, roughly chopped
6 garlic cloves, roughly chopped
3 cups cherry tomatoes
3 cups fresh basil

Preheat oven to 400 degrees F. Grease a large baking dish with 1 tablespoon of olive oil.

HALIBUT
Pat halibut fillets dry and lightly season both sides with salt and pepper. In a food processor, blend sundried tomatoes in oil and bread crumbs. Transfer mixture to a large bowl. Roll one side of each halibut fillet into bread crumb mixture, forming a layer of crust on the top. Place halibut fillets into baking dish and bake until fish is opaque, about 14 to 18 minutes.

YELLOW HEIRLOOM TOMATO SAUCE
Preheat the oven to 400 F. Grease a baking dish with 1 tablespoon of olive oil. Place yellow tomatoes, shallots and celery on baking dish. Lightly sprinkle with salt and pepper, to taste. Roast for 15 to 20 minutes or until tender. Cool. Remove skin from the tomatoes. Place all ingredients in a blender and puree until smooth. Strain to a smooth consistency.

CHERRY TOMATOES
In a large sauté pan, over moderate heat, sauté 3 tablespoons of olive oil, garlic, cherry tomatoes and basil for approximately 3 minutes or until tomatoes are softened but still whole. *Note: be very careful to gently toss the cherry tomatoes to prevent them from opening.

CREATE YOUR PLATE
Place cherry tomatoes onto the center of a plate. Place halibut fillet (crust side up) on top of the tomatoes. Drizzle yellow heirloom tomato sauce around the plate.

Chef's Tip:

If the cherry tomatoes start to open when cooked, you've cooked them too long!

PAN ROASTED CHILEAN SEA BASS

SERVES SIX

6 Sea Bass Fillets, about 6 ounces each
Sea salt
White pepper
8 tablespoons extra virgin olive oil, divided
1 whole shallot, finely diced
2 cups white wine, chardonnay
1-1/2 cups butter, softened
3 large heirloom tomatoes, cut lengthwise in half
3 cups mixed greens
1 teaspoon fresh lemon juice

Preheat oven to 350 degrees F. Grease a large baking sheet with cooking spray.

SEA BASS
Season fish fillets on both sides with salt and pepper. In a large saute pan, heat 3 tablespoons olive oil over medium-high heat. Add fillets to the pan and fry until done, about 4 minutes on each side. Arrange in baking sheet and finish in oven, about 3 to 6 minutes.

WHITE WINE BEURRE BLANC SAUCE
In a small saucepan, heat 3 tablespoons olive oil over medium-high heat. Add shallots and sauté until tender, about 10 minutes. Slowly stir in white wine.   Reduce heat and simmer, stirring often, until the mixture reduces by one-half, about 30 minutes. Cover sauce and cool to room temperature. Add butter and whisk until creamy.

MIXED GREEN SALAD
Place mixed greens in a large bowl. Drizzle with 2 tablespoons olive oil, lemon juice and salt and pepper, to taste.

CREATE YOUR PLATE
Ladle beurre blanc sauce onto a plate. Carefully place sea bass fillet on top of the sauce. Top 1 sliced tomato with ½ cup mixed green salad. Arrange tomato next to the fillet.

poultry

Tandoori Chicken WITH COCONUT SAUCE

Quail WITH RED CHERRIES

Kung Pao Chicken (THAI STYLE)

ORGANIC Grilled Chicken IN MUSHROOM SAUCE

MUSHROOM Stuffed Chicken

SWEET AND SOUR Chicken

CRISPY Thai Duck

DUCK a L'orange

Tandoori Chicken with Coconut Sauce

SERVES SIX

6 boneless, skinless chicken breasts, about 6 ounces each
3 cans unsweetened coconut milk
3 cups tandoori paste
2 limes, cut in half

CHICKEN
Preheat oven to 250 degrees F. Cut chicken into cubes. Place chicken on a broiler pan. Bake in the oven until the chicken is done, about 15 minutes.

COCONUT SAUCE
In a large saucepan, combine coconut milk and tandoori paste. Stirring constantly, bring to a slow simmer, and cook for about 5 minutes.

TANDOORI CHICKEN WITH COCONUT SAUCE
In a large bowl, combine chicken with coconut sauce. Toss evenly to coat.

CREATE YOUR PLATE
Place Tandoori Chicken onto a large serving platter and serve family style. Garnish with limes.

Chef's Tip:

Buy a jar of mango chutney at your local market; it tastes great with the chicken!

QUAIL WITH RED CHERRIES

SERVES SIX

Chef's Tip:

Substitute any berries that are in season.

3 cups balsamic vinegar
2 cups honey
1 tablespoon butter
3 cups fresh or frozen cherries, pitted
2 tablespoons cherry brandy
12 quails
2 tablespoons extra-virgin olive oil
Sea salt
White pepper

BALSAMIC REDUCTION
In a saucepan, add balsamic and honey. Bring to a slow boil, stirring often, until the mixture becomes a glaze.

WARMED CHERRIES IN BRANDY
In a large sauté pan, heat butter over moderate heat. Add cherries and brandy. Sauté until just tender.

QUAIL
Rub quails with olive oil and season with salt and pepper, to taste. Heat a large sauté pan over high heat. Add quail to the pan and brown until done.

CREATE YOUR PLATE
Ladle a spoonful of balsamic reduction onto the center of a plate. Place warmed cherries in brandy on top of the balsamic reduction. Position 2 quails back to back on top of the cherries.

Kung Pao Chicken (Thai Style)

SERVES SIX

3 cups roasted cashew nuts
Canola oil, for frying
2 pounds chicken breast, cut into thin strips
Sea salt
White pepper
2 cups cornstarch, more if needed
3 tablespoons extra-virgin olive oil
¼ cup garlic, peeled and chopped
Dried chilies cut into 1 centimeter pieces, to taste
1 each red, green and yellow bell peppers, cut into triangles
2 cups green onions, roughly chopped
2 tablespoons soy sauce
1 cup oyster sauce

CASHEW NUTS
Preheat oven to 250 degrees F. Toast the cashew nuts on a baking
sheet until golden brown, about ten minutes.

CHICKEN
Heat the canola oil in a very large, deep pot or heat an electric fryer
to 360 degrees F.   Season chicken with salt and pepper, to taste.
Lightly dredge the chicken in cornstarch. Fry the chicken, in batches,
until cooked and golden brown. Drain on paper towels.

VEGETABLES
In a large sauté pan, heat olive oil over moderate heat. Add garlic
and sauté until fragrant. Add chilies, peppers, onions and salt and
pepper, to taste.

CREATE YOUR PLATE
In a large serving bowl, combine chicken with vegetables. Add
soy sauce, oyster sauce and cashew nuts. Toss gently to combine.
Serve family style.

Chef's Tip:

*This dish pairs
nicely with
jasmine rice,
or long grain
white rice.*

Organic Grilled Chicken
in Mushroom Sauce

SERVES SIX

6 boneless, skinless, organic chicken breasts, about 5 to 6 ounces each
Sea salt
White pepper
2 tablespoon extra virgin olive oil, divided
1 tablespoon fresh thyme, finely minced
2 tablespoons butter
3 cloves garlic, roughly chopped
15 shallots, divided
3 cups Shitake mushrooms
1 cup white wine
1 cup heavy cream
18 strips of raw bacon
18 pearl onions

CHICKEN
Heat an outdoor grill or indoor grill pan to medium-high heat.
Season chicken breasts with salt and pepper, to taste, and rub with
1 tablespoon of olive oil. Sprinkle with thyme. Grill until grill marks
have formed and chicken is cooked through, about 5 minutes per side.

MUSHROOM SAUCE
In a large saucepan, heat butter over moderate heat. Add garlic
and 3 shallots (finely chopped), and sauté until caramelized. Add
mushrooms and sauté until tender. Add white wine, and stirring
often, reduce liquid by one-half. Add cream and reduce by one-half.
Transfer ingredients to a blender and puree until smooth.

BACON, SHALLOTS AND PEARL ONIONS
Slice bacon into small pieces. In a large skillet heat 1 tablespoon of
olive oil over medium-high heat. Add the bacon, 12 whole shallots and
18 pearl onions. Sauté until tender, about 12 minutes.

CREATE YOUR PLATE
Ladle a spoonful of mushroom sauce onto the center of a plate.
Portion the bacon mixture on top of the mushroom sauce. Place
1 chicken breast on top.

MUSHROOM STUFFED CHICKEN

SERVES SIX

6 tablespoons softened butter, divided
2 cups Shitake mushrooms
2 cups White Button mushrooms
2 cups Portobello mushrooms
5 sprigs of fresh thyme
White wine, splash
Sea salt
White pepper
6 boneless chicken breasts with skin, about 6 ounces each
6 leeks, finely diced
2 tablespoons extra virgin olive oil
½ cup heavy cream

MUSHROOMS
In a large sauté pan, heat 3 tablespoons butter over moderate heat.
Add mushrooms, thyme, white wine, and salt and pepper, to taste.
Cook until the mushrooms are tender. Remove from heat and cool
to room temperature.

CHICKEN
Preheat oven to 350 degrees F. Grease a large baking dish with 1
tablespoon of butter. Season the chicken with salt and pepper, to
taste. Stuff about 3 tablespoons of the mushroom mixture under the
skin of each chicken breast. Rub 2 tablespoons of butter on top of
the chicken breasts. Place chicken skin side up in the baking dish.
Bake until the chicken is cooked through, about 12 to 15 minutes.

LEEKS
In a large sauté pan, over medium-high heat, sauté leeks in olive-oil
until softened. Add cream and reduce heat to a slow simmer until
the cream evaporates.

CREATE YOUR PLATE
Place leeks onto the center of a plate. Arrange 1 chicken breast on
top of the leeks.

Chef's Tip:

*Use the
leftover cream
from the leeks
and drizzle
around the
plate.*

SWEET AND SOUR CHICKEN

SERVES SIX

1-20 ounce can pineapple chunks, drained
1 cup ketchup
1 cup sugar
½ cup white wine vinegar
6 skinless, boneless chicken breasts, julienned
2 cups cornstarch, more if needed
Canola oil, for frying
3 tablespoons extra virgin olive oil
2 tablespoons garlic, crushed
1 white onion, julienned
1 each red, yellow and green bell pepper, cut into triangles
1 cucumber, peeled and cubed
2 cups cup bean sprouts, divided
1/2 cup green onions, finely sliced

SWEET AND SOUR SAUCE
Drain the pineapple chunks, reserving 1 cup of the juice. In a large saucepan over moderate heat, simmer pineapple juice, ketchup, sugar, and white wine vinegar until done, about 20 minutes.

CHICKEN
Lightly dredge chicken in cornstarch, making sure it is completely coated. Heat the canola oil in a very large, deep pot or heat an electric fryer to 360 degrees F. Fry the chicken, in batches, until cooked and golden brown. Drain on paper towels.

SWEET AND SOUR CHICKEN
Heat olive oil in a large sauté pan over moderate heat. Add garlic, onions and peppers, and sauté until tender. Add chicken, pineapple chunks, cucumbers, 1 cup of bean sprouts, and sweet and sour sauce. Toss evenly to coat all the ingredients.

CREATE YOUR PLATE
Place sweet and sour chicken onto a large serving platter. Garnish with 1 cup of bean sprouts and green onions.

CRISPY THAI DUCK

SERVES SIX

6 duck breasts, about 6 ounces each
3 oranges, peeled, seeded, and blended
1 tablespoon soy sauce
1 tablespoon cornstarch
2 tablespoons extra-virgin olive oil
3 cups cooked Jasmine Thai Rice
1 each red, yellow and green bell pepper, julienned
½ white onion, julienned
Canola oil, for frying
½ cup fresh ginger, finely julienned (optional)

Chef's Tip:

Substitute any rice that you like best!

DUCK BREAST
Preheat oven to 350 degrees F. Heat a grill pan over medium-high heat. Cook duck breasts skin side down until crispy. Flip duck breasts over and cook for 2 more minutes. Transfer duck breasts to a baking dish. Place in the oven and bake until desired doneness.

ORANGE SAUCE
In a sauté pan, over moderate heat, combine blended oranges with soy sauce. Bring to a boil. Slowly add in the cornstarch and whisk until the sauce thickens.

RICE WITH VEGETABLES
In a large sauté pan, heat the olive oil over medium heat. Add rice, peppers and onions. Toss all ingredients until warm. Remove from heat.

FRIED GINGER (OPTIONAL)
In a small, deep saucepan, heat canola oil. Add ginger and flash-fry until crispy, about 30 seconds. Remove ginger and drain on paper towels.

CREATE YOUR PLATE
Spoon orange sauce onto the center of a plate. Place rice and vegetable mixture on top of the orange sauce. Layer 1 duck breast on top. Garnish with fried ginger.

Duck a L'Orange

3 large potatoes
2 garlic cloves, finely chopped
2 cups heavy cream
Sea salt
White pepper
4 tablespoons butter, divided
3 tablespoons brown sugar
4 granny smith apples, cored, peeled, and thinly sliced
1 cup granulated sugar
2 cups orange juice, freshly squeezed
½ cup red wine
½ cup fresh ginger, grated
6 duck breasts, about 6 ounces each
3 oranges, peeled, seeded and diced

CREAMY ROASTED POTATOES
Preheat oven to 350 degrees F. Peel and thinly slice potatoes and place in a large bowl. Add garlic, heavy cream and salt and pepper, to taste. Mix well, coating all the potatoes with cream. Grease a baking dish with 2 tablespoons of butter. Arrange the potatoes inside the baking dish. Cover with foil. Bake until done, about 45 minutes.

CARAMELIZED APPLES
In a large sauté pan, over medium-high heat, sauté 2 tablespoons of butter and brown sugar until completely melted. Add apples and sauté until caramelized, about 2 to 3 minutes.

ORANGE GINGER GLAZE
In a large, heavy saucepan, over high heat, caramelize 1 cup sugar. Add orange juice, wine and ginger. Reduce heat to a slow simmer and cook the liquid until reduced by one-half.

DUCK
Season the duck with salt and pepper, to taste. In a large sauté pan, over medium-high heat, cook the duck to desired doneness. Slice each duck breast into eight slices for a total of 48 slices.

CREATE YOUR PLATE
Stack potatoes in the center of a plate. Carefully over-lap 8 lamb slices and 8 apple slices over the potatoes. Drizzle Orange Ginger Glaze around the plate. Garnish with diced oranges.

meats

RANCHO SANTA FE Fillet

HOISIN CRUSTED Peppered Lamb

Fried Fillet Mignon AND EGG

Veal Loin WITH RED CURRANT SAUCE

Lamb with MINT RISOTTO

Pork with SWEET ORANGE CHILI SAUCE

Fillet MIGNON

Roasted Rack of Lamb IN HERB CRUST

Steak DIJON

Fillet Mignon WITH BONE MARROW

PENANG Beef Curry

Lamb STEW

Rancho Santa Fe Fillet

SERVES SIX

4 tablespoons unsalted butter, divided
3 cups fresh green peas
6 large morel mushrooms
18 chanterelle mushrooms
6 purple wax beans
1 cup chicken broth
Brandy, splash
6 fillets mignon, about 5 to 6 ounces each, cut about 1-inch thick
3 tablespoons extra-virgin olive-oil, divided
Sea Salt
White pepper
1 teaspoon rosemary
1 teaspoon fresh sage, finely minced
1 teaspoon fresh tarragon, finely minced
1 teaspoon fresh Italian parsley, finely minced
1 teaspoon Thai basil, finely minced

GREEN PEA AND MUSHROOM RAGU
Heat 2 tablespoons butter in a large sauté pan, over medium-high heat. Add peas, mushrooms, wax beans, chicken broth and a splash of brandy. Sauté until the mushrooms are tender, but not overcooked, about 5 to 6 minutes.

FILLET MIGNON
Season both side of the fillets mignon with 2 tablespoons olive oil, salt and pepper, to taste and fresh herbs. Melt 2 tablespoons of butter and 1 tablespoon of olive oil in a large, heavy skillet over medium-high heat. Cook fillets to desired doneness, about 3 minutes per side for medium-rare. Remove fillets to a serving platter and cover tightly with aluminum foil.

CREATE YOUR PLATE
Spoon green pea and mushroom ragu in the center of a plate. Position 1 fillet mignon on top of ragu.

Chef's Tip:

Keep an eye on the peas, making sure they don't overcook and become too soft.

HOISIN CRUSTED PEPPERED LAMB

SERVES SIX

18 lamb chops
3 tablespoons hoisin sauce plus ¼ cup, divided
4 tablespoons peppercorns
2 tablespoons soy sauce
3 tablespoons ginger, finely minced
4 tablespoons garlic, finely minced, divided
2 tablespoons sesame oil
3 tablespoons black sesame seeds
3 tablespoons white toasted sesame seeds
1 Thai chili, minced
2 tablespoons extra virgin olive oil
6 cups fresh baby spinach
½ cup coconut milk

MARINATED LAMB CHOPS
In a large bowl, combine 3 tablespoons hoisin sauce, peppercorns, soy sauce, ginger, 3 tablespoons garlic, sesame oil, sesame seeds and Thai chilies. Mix well. Add the lamb chops to the hoisin mixture and coat completely. Cover the bowl with plastic wrap and refrigerate overnight.

BAKED LAMB CHOPS
Preheat oven to 250 degrees F. Arrange the lamb chops on a wire rack inside a baking dish. Bake until desired doneness, about 10 to 12 minutes.

SPINACH
In a large sauté pan, heat olive oil and 1 tablespoon of garlic over medium-high heat. Add spinach and sauté until tender, about 5 to 10 minutes.

CREATE YOUR PLATE
Spoon spinach onto the center of a plate. Arrange three lamb medallions on top of the spinach. Drizzle hoisin sauce and coconut milk around the plate.

Fried Fillet Mignon and Egg

Serves Six

3 tablespoons extra-virgin olive oil
3 tablespoons minced garlic
1 yellow onion, julienned
2 green chilies, julienned
1 red chili, julienned
2 pounds filet mignon, diced
2 cups beef broth
3 teaspoons light soy sauce
½ cup oyster sauce
2 tablespoons sugar
6 cups green Thai basil
18 basil leaves
Canola oil, for frying
6 eggs, fried to your liking

FILLET MIGNON MIXTURE
Heat extra-virgin olive oil in a wok or sauté pan over medium high-heat. Add garlic, onions and chilies and sauté for 2 minutes or until golden brown. Add fillet mignon and sauté for one minute stirring continuously. Add beef broth and simmer for 2 minutes. Add soy sauce, oyster sauce and sugar. Continue to simmer until the beef is cooked. Add Thai basil leaves and toss gently until all the ingredients are evenly mixed.

FRIED BASIL LEAVES
Heat the canola oil in a small, deep pot. Flash-fry basil leaves in canola oil until crispy, about 1 minute. Remove leaves and drain on paper towels.

CREATE YOUR PLATE
Place fillet mignon mixture onto a plate. Place egg on top and garnish with 3 fried basil leaves.

Chef's Tips:

Holy basil leaves do not have a very strong flavor and are best used in large amounts to release the taste.

This dish is best eaten with Jasmine Thai or brown rice

VEAL LOIN WITH RED CURRANT SAUCE

SERVES SIX

2 red bell peppers
2 orange bell peppers
1 sheet brik pastry dough or 12 wonton skins
2-1/2 pounds of Veal loin cut into 12 pieces
2 tablespoons extra virgin olive oil
2 cups granulated sugar
4 cups red currant puree
2 cups red wine

ROASTED BELL PEPPERS
Preheat oven to 425 degrees F. Cover a heavy baking sheet with foil and coat with cooking spray. Arrange peppers on baking sheet and bake until the skins brown and blister, turning the peppers over occasionally, about 20 to 25 minutes. Place peppers in a bowl, cover with plastic wrap and allow to cool; about 10 minutes. Peel, seed and cut peppers into 18 circles.

PASTRY-WRAPPED VEAL LOIN
Preheat oven to 250 degrees F. Divide brik pastry (or wonton skins) into 12 small sheets. Wrap 1 veal loin in each of the sheets, forming a roll. Place on a large baking sheet greased with olive oil. Bake until done, about 8 to 10 minutes.

RED CURRANT SAUCE
Place sugar in a large saucepan. Stirring constantly, cook the sugar over medium-high heat until caramelized, making sure the sugar doesn't burn. Slowly add red currant puree and wine. Reduce to a slow simmer and cook until the liquid is reduced by less than one-half.

CREATE YOUR PLATE
Ladle red currant sauce onto a plate. Alternating colors, arrange 3 pepper slices around the plate. Top with 2 pastry-wrapped veal loins.

LAMB WITH MINT RISOTTO

SERVES SIX

6 lamb porterhouse chops, about 4 to 5 ounces each
Sea salt
White pepper
2 tablespoons extra-virgin olive oil
3 cups fresh mint
½ cup white wine
3 cups cooked risotto
5 egg yolks
2 tablespoons fresh lemon juice
2 teaspoons Worcestershire sauce
4 cups clarified butter
2 tablespoons fresh or dried tarragon

LAMB
Season lamb chops with salt and pepper, to taste. Brush chops on both sides with olive oil. Heat an outdoor grill or indoor grill pan over high heat. Grill chops until golden brown, or to desired doneness, about 3 to 4 minutes on each side.

MINT RISOTTO
In a blender combine mint with white wine. Puree until smooth. Place risotto in a large bowl. Slowly stir in mint mixture. Toss well.

BEARNAISE SAUCE
In the top of double broiler set over simmering water, whisk the egg yolks, lemon juice, and Worcestershire until very smooth. Add the butter, 1 cup at a time, until all is incorporated. Remove from heat. Add tarragon and salt and pepper, to taste. Mix well.

CREATE YOUR PLATE
Ladle Béarnaise sauce onto the center of a plate followed by ½ cup of mint risotto. Place 1 lamb chop on top of the risotto. Drizzle extra Béarnaise sauce around the plate.

PORK WITH SWEET ORANGE CHILI SAUCE

12 pork chops, about 5 ounces each
Sea salt
White pepper
2 tablespoons of extra virgin olive-oil
3 cups freshly squeezed orange juice
½ cup Thai chili sauce
2 tablespoons rice wine vinegar
2 tablespoons sugar

PORK CHOPS
Season pork chops with salt and pepper, to taste. Brush chops on both sides with olive oil. Heat an outdoor grill or indoor grill pan over high heat. Grill chops until cooked and golden brown, about 5 minutes on each side.

SWEET ORANGE CHILI SAUCE
In a large bowl combine orange juice, Thai chili sauce, vinegar and sugar. Whisk well.

CREATE YOUR PLATE
Ladle sweet orange chili sauce onto a plate. Place 2 pork chops on top.

FILLET MIGNON

6 Idaho potatoes
5 tablespoons butter, divided
2 cups morel mushrooms
2 cups chanterelle mushrooms, chopped
1 tablespoon garlic, finely minced
1 tablespoon chopped parsley
6 fillets mignon, about 5 to 6 ounces each
2 tablespoons extra-virgin olive oil
Sea salt
White pepper
3 whole shallots, roughly chopped
3 red tomatoes, roughly chopped
1 bottle port wine
3 cups of beef stock
1 black truffle, finely diced

POTATOES
Peel and cut potatoes into large cubes. Bring a large pot of salted water to a boil. Add potatoes and blanch, about 5 minutes. Remove potatoes and place in a bowl of ice water. Heat 3 tablespoons of butter in a large sauté pan over medium-high heat. Add potatoes, mushrooms, garlic and parsley. Stirring constantly, sauté until the potatoes are golden brown and the mushrooms are cooked al dente, about 5 minutes.

FILLETS MIGNON
Rub both side of the fillets with olive oil and season with salt and pepper, to taste. Heat a large sauté pan over high heat. Place fillets in the pan and cook to desired doneness, about 3 minutes per side for medium-rare. Remove fillets to a serving platter and cover tightly with aluminum foil.

PORT WINE TRUFFLE SAUCE
In a large sauté pan, heat 2 tablespoons butter over moderate heat. Add shallots and tomatoes and cook until caramelized. Add wine and beef stock. Bring to a slow simmer and reduce by one-half, until thick. Cool. Add truffles and mix well.

CREATE YOUR PLATE
Ladle port wine truffle sauce onto a plate. Place 1 fillet mignon in the center of the sauce. Portion cubed potatoes around the plate.

Chef's Tip:

Rub the fillets vigorously with the olive oil. This will release some of the fat and prevent the meat from burning.

ROASTED RACK OF LAMB
IN HERB CRUST

SERVES SIX

1 tube polenta
2 cups chicken broth
1 jar of fire roasted red bell peppers
1-1/2 cups finely minced yellow onions, divided
7 tablespoons extra-virgin olive oil, divided
3 garlic cloves, finely minced
1 whole eggplant, finely chopped
1 each red pepper, yellow pepper and orange pepper, finely chopped
1-14.5 ounce can tomato sauce
1 tablespoon fresh thyme, roughly chopped
1 tablespoon fresh parsley, roughly chopped
¼ cup white wine
1 tablespoon butter
6 lamb chops (bone-in and Frenched, about 4 ounces each)
2 cups bread crumbs
1 cup fresh parsley
1 cup fresh tarragon
Sea salt
White pepper

POLENTA
*Note: follow the package directions for preparation. You will need 12 slices of polenta (2 per plate).

FIRE ROASTED RED BELL PEPPER SAUCE
In a large saucepan combine chicken broth, 1 jar of peppers and ½ cup onions. Bring to a boil. Reduce to moderate heat and simmer until all the flavors are released, about 10 minutes. Cool and transfer in batches to a blender. Puree until smooth.

VEGETABLE RATATOUILLE
Heat 2 tablespoons of olive oil in a large skillet over medium-high heat. Add garlic, 1 cup onions, eggplant and peppers. Sauté until vegetables are crisp-tender, about 2 to 3 minutes.   Add tomato sauce, thyme, parsley, white wine and butter. Bring heat to a slow simmer and cook until the liquid is reduced by one-half, about 15 minutes.

HERB CRUSTED LAMB

Preheat oven to 350 degrees F. In a food processor, blend the bread crumbs, parsley, tarragon and 2 tablespoons of olive oil. *Note: if the crust is too dry, add more olive oil. Place in a large bowl and season with salt and pepper, to taste. Rub lamb chops with 2 table-spoons olive oil and roll in herb crust, pressing crust firmly onto the surface of both sides. Place chops on a large baking sheet coated with 1 tablespoon of olive oil.   Bake until medium-rare, about 10 minutes.

CREATE YOUR PLATE

Place 1 polenta circle on the side of a plate with vegetable Ratatouille on top. Top with another polenta circle. Place 1 lamb chop to the side of the polenta. Drizzle pepper sauce around the plate.

STEAK DIJON

SERVES SIX

6 top sirloin steaks, about 6 ounces each
Sea salt
White pepper
2 tablespoons extra-virgin olive oil
2 tablespoons Dijon mustard
1 cup breadcrumbs
12 leeks cut lengthwise
2 cups chicken broth
2 tablespoons butter
1 shallot, finely diced
2 cups fresh or frozen huckleberries
2 cups red wine
½ cup granulated sugar

STEAKS
Preheat the oven to broil. Rub steaks with olive oil and season with
salt and pepper, to taste. Brush Dijon on one side of each steak,
then top with breadcrumbs. Heat a large, heavy skillet to medium-
high. Cook the steaks to desired doneness, about 3 minutes per side
for medium-rare. Place steaks on a broiler pan and broil in the oven
until the crust is golden brown, about 1 minute.

LEEKS
Preheat oven to 350 degrees F. Place leeks inside a baking dish.
Add chicken broth. Cover and bake in the oven for 45 minutes
until tender.

HUCKLEBERRY SAUCE
Melt butter in a large saucepan over moderate heat. Add shallots
and cook until tender. Add huckleberries, wine and sugar. Bring to
a slow simmer and reduce liquid by one-half. Transfer to a blender
and puree until smooth.

CREATE YOUR PLATE
Ladle huckleberry sauce onto a plate. Arrange leeks on top of the
sauce. Place 1 steak on top of the leeks.

FILLET MIGNON WITH BONE MARROW

SERVES SIX

6 beef marrow bones
Sea salt
White pepper
6 wonton wrappers
6 tablespoons foie gras terrine
Canola oil, for frying
6 fillets mignon, about 6 ounces each, cut 2 inches thick
2 tablespoons extra virgin olive oil
6 sprigs rosemary
3 cups mashed potatoes
6 rosemary sprigs
6 tablespoons balsamic vinegar

MARROW BONES
Preheat oven to 450 degrees F. Drop bones in a large pot of boiling water and boil for 30 minutes on medium heat. Remove bones and put in a baking dish and cook for an additional 30 minutes. Season with salt and pepper, to taste.

FOIE GRAS WONTONS
Place 1 tablespoon of foie gras terrine in one wonton and fold closed. Repeat for remaining 5 wontons. Heat the canola oil in a small, deep saucepan. Flash-fry wontons until crispy, about 1 minute. Drain on paper towels.

FILLETS MIGNON
Preheat oven to 450 degrees F. Rub fillets with olive oil and season with salt and pepper, to taste. Heat an outdoor grill or indoor grill pan to high heat. Cook the fillets until crispy, about 3 minutes per side. Place fillets in a baking dish and finish in the oven until medium-rare, about 5 minutes.

CREATE YOUR PLATE
Spoon mashed potatoes onto the center of a plate. Place fillet mignon on top of potatoes. Garnish with foie gras wonton and 1 sprig of rosemary. Drizzle balsamic vinegar around the plate.

PENANG BEEF CURRY

SERVES SIX

4 (15-ounce) cans unsweetened coconut milk
1-1/2 cups Penang curry paste
4 teaspoons Thai nam pla, or Vietnamese nuoc nam (fish sauce)
2-1/2 cups granulated sugar
2 tablespoons extra-virgin olive oil
2 pounds filet mignon, thinly sliced
1 Thai eggplant, cubed
1 white onion, thinly sliced
2 cups fresh green peas
8 cups sweet basil, whole
3 fresh chilies thinly sliced, optional

CURRY SAUCE
In a large bowl, combine coconut milk, curry paste, fish sauce and sugar. Whisk well.

BEEF AND VEGETABLES
In a large saucepan, heat the olive oil over medium-high heat. Add the beef, eggplant, and onions. Cook until the meat is done, about 5 minutes. Remove from heat. Add the peas, basil and chilies. Pour in curry sauce and toss well to combine.

CREATE YOUR PLATE
Place Penang Beef Curry onto a large platter and serve family style.

Chef's Tips:

Pork, chicken, shrimp or tofu can be substituted for the beef.

Feel free to substitute regular eggplant for the Thai eggplant.

LAMB STEW

Lamb loin, cubed, about 5 pounds
4 large carrots, cubed
4 potatoes, cubed
1 yellow onion, cubed
8 cups beef broth
1 bottle red wine
6 bay leaves
Sea salt
White pepper

LAMB STEW
Combine all the ingredients into a large pot. Bring to a slow boil.
Once boiling, decrease the heat to low and simmer until the liquid is
absorbed and the lamb is tender, about 3 to 4 hours. Five minutes
before the stew is finished, add salt and pepper, to taste.

CREATE YOUR PLATE
Ladle the lamb stew into bowls.

desserts

BUTTERSCOTCH **Pudding**

CHERRIES **Jubilee**

Prune TART

Espresso Jelly WITH COFFEE ANGLAISE

CHOCOLATE **Wontons**

Sticky Rice WITH FRESH MANGO

CHOCOLATE **Lava Cake**

Créme BRULEE

Strawberries WITH ORANGE PINK PEPPERCORN SAUCE

BUTTERSCOTCH PUDDING

SERVES SIX

1 cup whole milk
3-1/2 cups heavy cream
½ cup granulated sugar
½ cup brown sugar
1 cup softened butter
5 egg yolks
2 tablespoons baking powder
2 tablespoons brandy
1 jar butterscotch sauce
1 jar hot fudge sauce

CREAM MIXTURE
In a large non-stick saucepan, combine milk, cream and sugars.
Bring to a slow boil, stirring constantly to dissolve the sugars.
Remove from heat.

EGG YOLK MIXTURE
In a medium bowl, combine butter, egg yolks, baking powder and
brandy. Whisk until smooth.

Add the egg yolk mixture to the cream mixture, whisking constantly
until very smooth. Bring to a slow simmer and cook until thick, about
5 to 7 minutes. Strain through a fine sieve into a large bowl. Cover
with plastic wrap and chill in the refrigerator for 4 to 6 hours.

CREATE YOUR PLATE
Spoon butterscotch sauce onto the center of a dessert plate. Spoon
pudding on top. Drizzle warm fudge over the pudding.

CHERRIES JUBILEE

3 cups cherries in brandy, drained, reserving 1 cup of the juice
2 cups cherry brandy
2 tablespoons cornstarch
1 pint berry sorbet

CHERRY SAUCE
In a sauté pan, over moderate heat, combine cherry juice, cherry brandy and cornstarch. Cook to a smooth and thick consistency, about 3 minutes.

CREATE YOUR PLATE
Ladle cherry sauce onto a plate. Arrange cherries around the plate. Garnish with berry sorbet.

Chef's Tip:

Use any sorbet of your choice.

PRUNE TART

SERVES SIX

1 cup softened, unsalted butter, divided
2 tablespoons brown sugar
18 prunes
1 cup golden raisins
1 cup raisins
1 cup brandy
48 puffed pastry sheets cut into 3x3 inch squares
6 tablespoons honey
3 cups vanilla ice-cream
½ cup fresh berries
½ cup shaved almonds

TART FILLING
In a large sauté pan, over low heat, sauté ½ cup butter, sugar, prunes, raisins and brandy until softened. Remove from heat and cool to room temperature.

Chef's Tip:

Be careful not to overcook the tarts.

PRUNE TARTS
Preheat oven to 350 degrees F. In a small sauté pan, melt ½ cup of butter. You will need 8-3x3 inch pastry squares per tart. Brush 1 pastry sheet with butter and repeat with 2 more sheets, stacking the 3 sheets on top of one another. Fill with 1 tablespoon of the tart filling. Repeat with 3 more pastry sheets brushed with butter and placed on top. Brush with more butter. Seal the tart by pressing gently on the edges. Place on a baking sheet and bake until light golden brown, about 12 to 15 minutes.

CREATE YOUR PLATE
Place prune tart onto a dessert plate. Drizzle with 1 tablespoon of honey. Garnish with ½ cup of vanilla ice-cream, fresh berries and almonds.

Espresso Jelly with Coffee Anglaise

SERVES SIX

6 gelatin molds
12 gelatin sheets
1 cup granulated sugar
1 cup water
2 cups strong black coffee
3 tablespoons rum
6 tablespoons coffee liqueur, divided
1 cup whole milk
1 cup heavy cream
6 tablespoons granulated sugar
5 egg yolks
6 tablespoons mascarpone cheese
1 teaspoon vanilla
4 large dates, julienned

GELATIN SHEETS
Place gelatin sheets in a small bowl. Add cold water and soak for about 3 minutes.

ESPRESSO JELLY
In a small saucepan, bring the sugar and water to a boil. Stirring constantly, dissolve the sugar completely. Add coffee, rum and 3 tablespoons of coffee liqueur. Remove gelatin sheets from the water and add to the mixture. Fill gelatin molds with the mixture and refrigerate for 4 hours.

COFFEE ANGLAISE
In a large saucepan, combine milk, cream, sugar and egg yolks. Whisking constantly, bring to a slow boil and cook for about 2 minutes. Reduce heat to low and add 3 tablespoons of coffee liqueur and cook until thickened, about 5 to 10 minutes. Strain to a smooth consistency and cool.

MASCARPONE CHEESE TOPPING
In a small bowl combine mascarpone cheese with vanilla. Mix well until creamy.

CREATE YOUR PLATE
Ladle coffee anglaise onto the center of a dessert plate. Gently swirl a butter knife around the edges of 1 espresso jelly mold and remove. Place espresso jelly on top of the coffee anglaise. Garnish with mascarpone cheese and dates.

CHOCOLATE WONTONS

SERVES SIX

Canola oil, for frying
6 wonton sheets, thawed
12 tablespoons chocolate chips
2 egg yolks, beaten
18 tablespoons chocolate sauce
6 tablespoons raspberry sauce

Heat the canola oil in a very large, deep pot or heat an electric fryer to 360 degrees F.

CHOCOLATE WONTONS
Cut wontons into 6 individual squares. Place 1 tablespoon of chocolate chips in the center of one wonton square. Fold into a triangle. Seal by brushing with egg yolk mixture. Repeat the process for the remaining 5 wonton squares. Lower wontons into the oil and deep fry until crispy and golden brown, about 3 minutes. Carefully transfer to drain on paper towels.

CREATE YOUR PLATE
Drizzle chocolate sauce onto the center of a dessert plate. Layer 1 wonton on top of the sauce. Drizzle raspberry sauce around the plate.

Sticky Rice with Fresh Mango

3 cups Jasmine Thai rice
2 cups sweetened coconut milk
2 tablespoons cornstarch
3 large mangos cut in half
1 pint fresh raspberries
6 sprigs of mint

RICE
Clean, rinse and drain the rice. Set up a bamboo steaming basket according to manufacturer's directions and transfer rice into the basket. Cover and reduce the heat to maintain a steady steam, and cook until the rice is sticky, about 30 to 45 minutes. Coat a large baking sheet with cooking spray. Gently spread the rice into a shallow layer onto the baking sheet. Refrigerate for at least 2 hours.

COCONUT SAUCE
In a large, heavy, non-stick saucepan, heat coconut milk over medium heat. Add cornstarch and cook until thickened. Remove from heat and cool. Pour coconut sauce over rice on the baking sheet and refrigerate for another hour.

CREATE YOUR PLATE
Spoon rice onto the center of a plate and arrange 1/2 mango on top. Garnish with raspberries and 1 sprig of mint.

CHOCOLATE LAVA CAKE

SERVES SIX

6 (6 ounce) ramekins
6 ounces chocolate chips
10 ounces unsalted butter, softened
5 egg yolks
6 eggs
1 1/4 cups sugar
1 1/4 cups flour all purpose flour, sifted
1 1/4 cups heavy whipping cream
4 tablespoons powdered sugar
1 1/4 teaspoons vanilla

Preheat oven to 350 degrees F.

CHOCOLATE MIXTURE
In a double boiler over medium-high heat, melt chocolate chips and butter. Remove from heat.

EGGS AND SUGER
In a large bowl, whisk together the egg yolks, eggs and sugar.

CHOCOLATE CAKE BATTER
Combine chocolate mixture with egg and sugar mixture. Fold in flour.

CHOCOLATE LAVA CAKES
Divide batter evenly among ramekins; filling them about 2/3 to 3/4 of the way full. Bake until cakes rise, about 10 to 15 minutes. The outside of the cake will form a crust, but the center should remain a thick liquid.

WHIPPED CREAM
In a large mixing bowl combine whipping cream, powdered sugar and vanilla. Using an electric mixer set on high speed; beat the cream until stiff peaks form.

CREATE YOUR PLATE
Garnish warm lava cake with a dollop of whipped cream.

Chef's Tip:

Garnish lava cake with vanilla bean ice-cream and a drizzle of hot fudge if you prefer!

CRÈME BRULEE

SERVES SIX

6 (6-ounce) ramekins or custard cups
1 cup whole milk
2 cups heavy cream
1 teaspoon vanilla
6 egg yolks
1-1/2 cups sugar, divided
½ cup light brown sugar
½ cup fresh blackberries
1 cup fresh raspberries
6 sprigs of mint

CUSTARD
In a large, heavy, non-stick saucepan, over low heat, combine milk, cream and vanilla. Stirring constantly, cook for 15 minutes. Remove from heat.

EGGS AND SUGAR
In a large mixing bowl, beat egg yolks with an electric mixer set on high speed, until light and fluffy, about 5 minutes. Gradually beat in 1 cup sugar. Add in the custard mixture, a little at a time, whisking until well blended.

BAKED CRÈME BRULEE
Preheat oven to 350 degrees F. Evenly divide custard into ramekins. Place ramekins in a large baking dish. Pour enough hot water into the baking dish to cover half of the ramekins. Bake until the crème brulee is almost set, about 30 to 35 minutes. Remove the ramekins from the baking dish and refrigerate for at least 2 hours. Remove the ramekins from the refrigerator for at least 30 minutes prior to browning the sugar on top.

SUGAR TOPPING
In a small bowl, combine ½ cup granulated sugar with ½ cup light brown sugar. Evenly divide sugar by sprinkling a thin layer over each custard, covering it completely. Place custard in the oven and caramelize the topping under the broiler. Allow the crème brulee to sit for at least 5 minutes before serving.

CREATE YOUR PLATE
Garnish crème brulee with fresh berries and 1 sprig of mint.

Chef's Tip:

When cooking the custard, make sure the heat is not too high or the custard will burn.

Strawberries with Orange Pink Peppercorn Sauce

SERVES SIX

2 cups sugar
1 cup water
3 cups orange juice
½ cup heavy cream
36 large fresh strawberries
3 cups mango sorbet
6 sprigs of mint

Chef's Tip:

Use any flavor of sorbet or ice-cream that you like best!

ORANGE PINK PEPPERCORN SAUCE
In a medium sauce-pan, over high heat, stir the water and sugar until caramelized. Add orange juice. Reduce heat to medium-low. Stirring constantly, reduce the liquid by one-half. Add the cream and continue stirring until thickened, about 5 minutes.

CREATE YOUR PLATE
Ladle orange pink peppercorn sauce onto a plate. Arrange six strawberries around the plate. Place a scoop of mango sorbet in the center. Garnish with 1 sprig of mint.

Kerman Beriker

Educated in Switzerland, Kerman Beriker has been a dedicated hotelier, manager and consultant for over forty years, providing only the very best service and hospitality from luxury hotels throughout the United States, Europe, Canada, Mexico, and the Caribbean.

Beriker was Vice President of Operations of Rosewood Hotels in Dallas, Texas. He was the General Manager of the Hotel Bel-Air, and for 10 years he was the Chief Executive Officer and General Manager of The Beverly Hills Hotel; bringing both hotels to a 'Five-Star' rating for the first time.

The Los Angeles Business Journal selected Beriker to be the 1995 recipient of the 'Executive of the Year' award and Mayor Allan Alexander of the City of Beverly Hills proclaimed March 19th, 1996 as 'Kerman Beriker Day'. He was also named 'one of the 10 Best Hoteliers in the world' by LEADERS Magazine in 1997.

Beriker is a member of the International Wine and Food Society and the Chaîne des Rôtisseurs. A devoted member of the Beverly Hills and Rancho Santa Fe Rotary International, he was selected 'Rotarian of the Year' in Rancho Santa Fe in 2005.

At present, Beriker is the Managing Director of The Inn at Rancho Santa Fe. In 2007, both he and The Inn received the Bagnall Award for Excellence in Philanthropy. "Having worked all around the world, managing The Inn is a delight beyond words," says Beriker. "The Inn is a paradise in the center of everything in this civilized and peaceful town; boasting stunning views of the Village of Rancho Santa Fe. It is extremely understated."

A.S.F. 23
5-23-22